Interventions

PostModernPositions
A Monograph Series in Cultural Studies

Robert Merrill and Pat Wilkinson-Bus, series editors

---

1. Robert Merrill, ed. *Ethics / Aesthetics: Post-Modern Positions.*

2. Stephen-Paul Martin, *Open Form and the Feminine Imagination: The Politics of Reading in Twentieth-Century Innovative Writing.*

3. Keith C. Pheby, *Interventions: Displacing the Metaphysical Subject.*

4. Douglas Kellner, ed. *Postmodernism / Jameson / Critique.*

Maisonneuve Press
Publications of the Institute for Advanced Cultural Studies
P. O. Drawer 2980
Washington, DC 20013-2980

Interventions

Displacing
the
Metaphysical
Subject

By

Keith C. Pheby

PostModernPositions,   Volume 3

 MAISONNEUVE PRESS

Publications of the Institute for Advanced Cultural Studies

Keith C. Pheby. *Interventions: Displacing the Metaphysical Subject.*

Copyright © 1988 by Maisonneuve Press,
P. O. Drawer 2980, Washington, DC 20013-2980

Maisonneuve Press is a division of the **Institute for Advanced Cultural Studies**, a non-profit collective of scholars and activists concerned with the critical study of culture. Write to the Director for information about Institute programs and activities of the Press.

Printed in the United States by BookCrafters, Chelsea, MI. This book has been designed and manufactured to meet the standards set forth by the Committee on Production Guidelines for Book Longevity of the Council on Library Resources.

Library of Congress Cataloging-in-Publication Data
Main entry under title:

Pheby, Keith C., 1952—
Interventions: displacing the metaphysical subject.

(PostModernPositions, v. 3)
Bibliography: p. 117-121
Includes index: p. 123-126

1. Subjectivity.　2. Heidegger, Martin, 1889-1976.　3. Derrida, Jacques.　4. Foucault, Michel.
I. Title. II. Series.

BD222.P48　1988　　　　　　　　126　　　　　　　　88-21523

ISBN 0-944624-04-9 (cloth, alk. paper)
ISBN 0-944624-05-7 (pbk., alk. paper)

Contents

To Delia

There is no support to be found and no depth to be had for this bottomless chessboard where being is set in play.

Introduction
Displacing the Metaphysical Subject

And perhaps to all those who strive above all to maintain the unity of the philosopher's grammatical function . . . we could oppose Bataille's exemplary enterprise: his desperate and relentless attack on the preeminence of the philosophical subject. His experience and his language become an ordeal, a deliberate drawing and quartering of that which speaks in philosophical language, a dispersion of stars that come out at midnight, voiceless words to be born. (Foucault, *Language, Counter-Memory, Practice* 42)

If this present critique of metaphysical notions of subjectivity is to be more than just another somewhat tiresome deconstructive sally for the amusement of the anti-academic strain in contemporary culture, then I must be successful in persuading the reader that there is more at stake than meets the eye. What that "more" amounts to, I shall be arguing, is the possibility of a *praxis*, unfettered by traditional predispositions concerning social-bonding—a *praxis*, therefore, the motivation for which lies in an awareness of our global predicament of nuclear and ecological devastation.

To what extent deconstructive strategies have a role to play in the practical arena is a highly explosive issue. While Jacques

Derrida continually refuses to ally himself with liberation movements, there is a marked reticence on his part to condemn or subject certain revolutionary postures to deconstructive analysis. Derrida does not want to weaken "what Marxism and the proletariat can constitute as a force in France" (Fraser, "French Derrideans" 128).

Inasmuch as deconstruction resists entrenchment, resists becoming defined univocally by the dominant culture, it cannot fail to constitute a transgressive posture when confronted with the hegemony of Western rationalism and its technological domination of the earth. Thus, as Gayatri Spivak has argued, the discourse of deconstruction cannot continue to exclude that of political economy (Fraser 130). To persist in reducing the latter to "the status of a pre-critical method duped by its own axiomatic" is to be duped oneself in turn. It is to fall back "into a pre-critical, ideological space" and to reproduce the very gesture of marginalization: exclusion. Any such marginalization ignores the most important political lesson to be learned from Derrida: theory is a practice. One must be careful "not to exclude the other term of a polarity or the margins of a center" (130); one must put in question the normative value of the institutions and disciplines in and by which we live. For Spivak, there can be no separation of deconstruction from a thoroughgoing critique of social relations. In similar fashion (as we shall see in detail in Part Two), Foucault argues that the relation between rationalization and the excesses of political power is evident and "we should not need to wait for bureaucracy or concentration camps to recognize the existence of such relations" ("Afterword" 210).

Thus, despite a certain reticence, not to say opposition from the deconstructive purist (if one can do anything with that notion), the space for a radical praxis has been opened up, and in a way that does not rely on a falling back into ideological posturing. Derrida is extremely careful not to fall into the hands of the academy. He attempts to prevent *différance* from becoming a transcendental concept by incessantly shifting its ground, as it were. Thus deconstruction is an ongoing work, not a position or a standpoint—but a praxis, an activity, an "exercise in disruption," as John Caputo puts it. The desire to focus on key terms such as *différance*, "supplement," "trace," or "hymen" as if they can be "pinned down" and given a univocal definition must be resisted. Derrida's deployment of these terms should not be seen as an attempt to produce a foundation for critical analysis. The terms themselves are not "superconcepts" but strategies, their function is to dislodge and displace the logical categories through which the "meaning" of the text is usually displayed. Thus, deconstruction does not "destroy" the text, rendering meaning an impossibility, but demonstrates that the text signifies in a variety of ways and with varying degrees of explicitness. To show that this is the case, Derrida must commit certain indiscretions with respect to the tradition.

Perhaps one of the most distressing of these indiscretions, from the standpoint of the "average" reader, is the overturning of the semantic in favor of the syntactic. As Barbara Johnson has stated, Derrida's grammar is often "unspeakable," his texts ambiguous ("Introduction" to *Dissemination*). This, of course, produces an unsettling effect on the reader who is attempting to recuperate meaning. But this is precisely the "effect" that Derrida wants. The strategy is to "shake up" the structure: to make it "tremble" (*ébranler*). Thus, Derrida will speak of *ébranler* in connection with "displacement" and with "solicitation." The etymology of the latter term shows that the word is derived from the Latin *citare* (to put in motion) and *sollus* (in archaic Latin, the whole). It is important to recognize that in classical rhetoric we move vertically from the sensible to the "spiritual"; the materiality of the signifier is subsumed under the ideality of the signified. Now, Derrida reverses the procedure: "style" and "ornament" for example are not periphera, are not mere embellishments of the text; they generate texts on a level that is non-representational.

I must insist again that the force of these strategies is not to negate meaning but to expose the structure that lies at the heart of any attempted univocal reading of the text. Furthermore, it must be pointed out that Derrida is not merely arguing for the notion of "polysemy" which would suggest that while there may be many possible signifieds for any given signifier, the range of such possibilities remains finite. Derrida is more radical. As Tom Conby has noted, with *dissemination* "the syntactical play of spacings does not limit polysemy to given combinations of phonemes" ("A Trace of Style" 50). The "free play" of syntactic elements is not restricted and controlled by an inherent rationale, internal to the syntactic elements themselves but by "ideological complicities" that are in correspondence between reader and text. But again, the word is *déplacement* and not *dépassement*. The effect is to show that the text is not an open book but always involves a productive act on the part of the reader. If univocity is the result of such a production, it is not generated by the limited possibilities of the text but by the imposition of certain logical categories.

It is precisely this exposure of ideology at work that gives deconstruction its force as a political praxis. One of the basic claims of deconstruction is that philosophical texts are not privileged in relation to literary texts. All texts, whether "scientific," "literary," "philosophical," or "political" can be a target for deconstruction. No pure or transparent sign exists, and the belief that there is depends upon a whole tradition of thinking that privileges "presence." Derrida's strategies produce at one and the same time a freeing of the repressed, the absent, the marginal, plus a critique of the center, the dominant voice, the univocal reading. The unmasking and demystification of unconscious or naturalized binary oppositions in contemporary and traditional thought, together with a demonstration that they grow out of a particular mode of disclosure (logocentrism or a metaphysics of presence) is of itself a formidable political weapon considering that the legitimation of the centrality of a particular term is effected by means of the marginalization of the inessential one. Given that my major aim is a critique of the metaphysical notion of subjectivity (*qua* rational consciousness) such a binary opposition as self / other appears as particularly pernicious inasmuch as the privileging of the "I" forces the other into the realm of the dependent and inessential.

So far we have spoken of "overturning" and "displacement," but can deconstruction also be "constructive?" If this means that deconstruction attempts to build new models of thought and action, then the anwser is "no"—it does not. However, we are not left dangling over the abyss. Part of the displacement of logocentrism concerns a refusal to acquiesce to the power of the center, a refusal to adopt the belief that the dominant structures somehow have a priviledged access to meaning and truth. Our concern, in the first instance, will be to privilege the marginal, yet this might seem to imply in the political sphere that one could affirm both the alternatives provided on the one hand by feminism and on the other by terrorism. While many will, I hope, be persuaded by the former, embracing the latter will undoubtedly be unacceptable. However, it is not the case that "anything goes" on the margins. The whole thrust of deconstructive strategies is to resist a univocal disclosure of "meaning," "truth," and "structure." Terrorism, although it also attempts to make the dominant structure "tremble," does so by deploying the very method of metaphysics itself. Invariably, the motives for terrorist acts are ideological; they rest upon notions such as the preservation of national identity (in the face of imperialism) or the protection of sovereignty. If, as I shall be arguing in due course, the dual notions of autonomy and sovereignty are the most pernicious of metaphysical postulates, they must be critiqued even if they appear at the margins of our culture. Any party which decides to adopt coercive and authoritarian measures as its standard mode of operation has thereby decided to constitute itself as an authoritarian institution. It goes almost without saying, violence is a radical type of "closure."

In this present study, I will argue that the current global political arena is fraught with danger: a danger that confronts not merely the modern technologized subject but the conditions for the possibility of all discourse and all future discourse. It is necessary that we transform social relations on a global basis—though, I hasten to add, I am not suggesting a "global totality" (a notion to be discussed in the final chapter). It is necessary to rethink political experience without recourse to the rational subject as the primary locus of signification and without the attendant notions of autonomy and sovereignty, whether of subject or nation—both are products of the metaphysics of presence which I seek to displace. At the heart of this retracing of the political is the nature of the social bond. Perhaps, if successful, this study will constitute a preface to the adumbration of an adequate notion of social relations which escapes both the stifling confines of essentialism, yet also avoids the somewhat trite (and perhaps impossible) disavowal of the political that one detects in much post-modernist writing. What then will be the structure of this critique of subjectivity?

Part One: Placing the Subject concerns the traditional problem of the constitution of the human subject. Despite its plurality of configurations, it could be argued that at its heart the metaphysical tradition constitutes a continuing attempt to capture the elusive nature of being *qua* being. If this quest is not to be frustrated, being must be construed as self-contained, self-identical—it must be fully present. Without this constraint it would be impossible, in traditional metaphysics, to method-ologically delimit a path to it. Thus, the "really real" must be motionless, for any notion of movement (*Bewegung* for Heidegger) would be an *ekstasis*, a standing out from its proper place. Similarly, the philosophical subject, particularly since the hegemony of the Cartesian *cogito*, is conceived as that self-identical center of certainty, the locus of truth. Chapter 1 constitutes a broad (albeit incomplete) survey of the ontological presuppositions evident in the "being-question" with respect to the Western philosophical tradition and how these presup-positions infuse the metaphysical notion of the subject which is to be critiqued. I will also include a brief discussion of the moral language of the tradition inasmuch as I will, of necessity, have to make recourse to at least one of its ethical terms—that of "responsibility."

I will argue that the "what am I" question, the quest for human essence, relies on the same metaphysical presuppositions as the search for the "intrinsic" nature of being. However, it could be said that Hegel's *Phenomenology of Spirit* represents the commencement of a radical shift of emphasis concerning the way we approach the question of subjectivity. The Hegelian insistence that selfhood is to be construed as a dynamic, thoroughly historical notion has done much to influence the current hermeneutic and deconstructive strategies. In this vein, Chapter 2 will examine Heidegger's existential analysis of *Dasein* and the attempt of fundamental ontology to radically broaden the analysis of selfhood to contain the existential facticity of the self, rather than dwelling exclusively on the constitution of consciousness, as we find in Husserl. It is here that the interrelation of the self, time, and language will be introduced as a primary theme of this study. It is precisely the forgetfulness of the intimate connection between the self and temporality that has allowed that particularly pernicious *Gestell* (mode of enframing), technology, to so successfully reify the self in terms of an efficiently normalized, organized object. Heidegger's entire project can be seen as an attempt to radically temporalize both being and subject, to deny to the metaphysical self the role of origin for the disclosure of being. The Heideggerian critique of the metaphysics of language, together with his insistence upon the temporalizing nature of poeticized discourse, helps situate the discussion of Derrida's deployment of *différance*, which, in many respects (as I shall argue) can be mapped onto Heidegger's conception of *Ereignis*, the appropriating event.

In **Part Two: Displacing the Subject,** the relation between self, language, and structure is addressed. Perhaps Heidegger, more than any other thinker of modern times, has realized the need to move beyond the philosophical limitations of "Enlightenment" thought, to look away from the cognitive subject in an attempt to understand what the human being is. His later writings constitute a total rejection of the philosophical primacy of the subject *qua* rational consciousness. Such an "anti-humanism" is developed, extended, and significantly modified under the auspices of "structuralism" and "post-structuralism." Heidegger's proclamation that "language speaks not man" attains greater emphasis in Derrida's post-Sausserian deconstructive strategies.

The subject is decentered and dislocated in favor of structure which is in turn displaced in favor of *différance*. Chapter 3, then, both considers Derrida's deployment of *différance* to disrupt logocentric categories and also introduces what I conceive as the political effects of such a deployment in the social sphere.

Deconstructive strategies do not take place in a political vacuum. The discursive formations that infuse the social body, organizing its surfaces, are the result of power-laden strategies of social control. Conceptions of subjectivity are generated by dominant discursive formations, positivities (knowledges) which constitute relations of power within particular cultures. The chapter called "The Self and Power" thus concerns Foucault's genealogical method. While deconstruction provides an invaluable tactic for undermining Western rationalism, genealogy, by mapping the current micrological power relations, provides a useful tool for a transgressive praxis. Only by understanding the way that power functions within the dominant structure will we be in a position to resist its effects, at least nullifying those effects which appear to us as particularly pernicious. Such a transgression (putting dominant power structures under erasure is always a transgressive act) requires a taxonomy of power relations. Indeed, Foucault is at times insistent that a new economy of power relations is precisely what is required.

> It consists of taking the forms of resistance against different forms of power as a starting point. To use another metaphor, it consists of using this resistance as a chemical catalyst so as to bring to light power relations, locate their position, find out their point of application and the methods used. ("Afterword" 211)

If, as Pierre Macherey has argued, at "the edge of every text one encounters the language of ideology" (*Theory of Literary Production* 60), then the most relevant way of diffusing the power of ideology is to understand its internal mechanism.

As I have already indicated, the primary purpose of this study is to adumbrate a notion of social bonding which avoids recourse to the metaphysical subject as the point of departure. This, of course, necessitates an overturning of any type of Hobbesian or Contract theses of social development as well as any notion of human beings that assigns to them a natural function. Both positions rely upon an *a priori* assumption which I shall critique: that of an autonomous, self-present subject. My impetus for the proposed cultural transformation is pragmatic in the broadest sense possible. It relies on the presupposition that global collapse through nuclear confrontation or ecological destruction is feasible. If we are to avoid these dire consequences, human sociality can no longer be defined in terms of ideological or national allegiances. Our technology forces us to be concerned with the Earth as a whole. Any ethical posture must seriously consider the radical interdependence of all the peoples of the Earth. The recognition of the role of the other in the constitution of selfhood is the first step in the process. When the other is construed widely enough to contain all those repressed discourses that are victims of the primacy of technological disclosure, such a recognition becomes also a mark of transgression with respect to the dominant culture. Deconstruction reveals what logocentrism conceals—domination—and the deconstructive posture reaches out to the exteriority of the absent, the other that the dominant culture relegates to the abyss of "non-being."

Thus, the final chapter will attempt to explicate in greater detail the notion of "global responsibility": a way of responding to the other which does not rely upon metaphysical categories such as those of duties and obligations, taken as an external relation holding between self and other. Furthermore, I will elaborate precisely what I mean by the term "global," given that certain objections may be levelled against deconstruction with respect to the notion of "totality." Some have argued that faced as we are with a "total problem," the possibility of devastation by nuclear war, we must formulate a total solution. What I show about "totality" or the "totalizing posture" is that it indicates metaphysics and must be resisted in our formulation of a transgressive praxis. The forms of resistance must be plural and incessant.

Let me conclude this introduction with a comment on my deployment of Derrida, Heidegger, and Foucault. There are, of course, substantive differences between them in their methodologies and teachings. Foucault's genealogies have often been viewed as a variety of positivism by the deconstructionists, and at times, Heidegger has been attacked by both Derrida and Foucault as a metaphysician. But despite these differences, they do exhibit an over-arching desire to deconstruct and oppose the metaphysics of presence. It is this point of coalescence that interests me. I shall be arguing later that if logocentrism is to be made to "tremble," then the modes of resistance must be multifarious. As such I shall not be concerned to demonstrate exact parallels between, for example, Heidegger's "destruction" of metaphysics, Derrida's deconstruction of texts and Foucault's genealogical analyses of "Enlightenment" thought. Rather, I will argue that each "position" has an inherently disruptive effect upon the dominant techno-metaphysical *Gestell*. Thus, despite the fact that Heidegger demarcates Nietzsche thoroughly within the metaphysical camp, a more "open" reading of Nietzsche's texts generates a Nietzsche that is far from metaphysical. In a similar fashion the Derridean critique of Heidegger seems to exhibit a certain forgetfulness of the pluralism of Heidegger's styles. The poetic, evocative and considerably dense style of work such as "Conversation on a Country Path" (in *Discourse on Thinking*) should not be read (unless one's project is to narrow Heidegger's thought) without the recognition that Heidegger is employing terms, such as "die Gegnet" (that-which-regions) in an attempt to circumvent the reification of being. Contrary to Spivak, I fail to see in what repect Heidegger's putting of being "under erasure" (*sous rature*) "might point at an inarticulable presence" ("Preface" to *Of Grammatology*).

But to return to Nietzsche for a moment. It does seem clear that what interests Derrida (and myself) is that the plurality of Nietzche's styles does disrupt logocentrism and free the signifier from its dependence upon "truth" and "meaning." For Nietzsche, philosophical discourse itself is to be deciphered and this includes (as with Derrida) a critique of its own presuppositions.

Now, I do not want to belabor this point but to stress that for my purposes the texts that I shall be deploying do not and need not admit of a univocal reading (no text, as we shall see shortly, is in that "ideal" position). We must learn to use and erase our language at the same time.

Part One

Placing the Subject

The Metaphysics of Presence

1. Being

> The history of Being is never past but stands ever before, it sustains and defines every *condition et situation humaine.* In order to learn how to experience the aforementioned essence of thinking purely, and that means at the same time to carry it through, we must free ourselves from the technical interpretation of thinking. The beginnings of that interpretation reach back to Plato and Aristotle. (Heidegger, *Basic Writings* 194)

To think the essence of being in a way appropriate to "its" nature has been both the task and the failure of the Western metaphysical tradition. Perhaps the most pervasive and fundamental flaw in Western thinking stems from the desire to know being in its totality, as if "it" could be confined, defined, and presented—ready for inspection. Heidegger's argument demonstrates that the Platonic separation of "essence" or "whatness" and "existence" or "thatness" leads to a construal of "being" as the essence of what exists (*End of Philosophy* 55). Thus, being is thought in terms of the ground of beings, as their first cause and thus as the highest being. As Joan Stambaugh has put it,

> The original meaning of existence as *physis*, orginating, arising, presencing, is lost, and existence is thought only in contrast to essence as what 'factually' exists. In contrast to what 'factually' exists here and now, Being is set up as permanent presence, a presence (nominal) abstracted from presencing (verbal) in terms of time-space.
> ("Introduction" to the *End of Philosophy* x)

Certain presuppositions are evident in this approach. First there is the belief that being is a whole: reality is one closed system characterized by terms such as "unity," order, etc. Second, there is a certain "forgetfulness" of time. The exclusive concern with the present has the effect of ignoring the primordial characteristics of time: "ontology supersedes time or levels it off to static time, i.e., eternity" (Poeggler, "Being as Appropriation" 85). The originary movement from absence to presence is lost.

In "Kant and the Closure of the Metaphysic of Presence," Cornay has argued with Heidegger that in the pre-Parmenidean Greek the primary verb "to be" is *einai*. It derives from the Indo-European *es* and exhibits a "systematic plurivocity." It can mean both to be "temporally-duratively" present, to be "locatively" present or situated in a place, and also to be present in "lightedness" or unconcealment—*aletheia*.

> What prior to everything else first grants unconcealment is the path on which thinking pursues one thing and perceives it: *hopos estin . . . einai*: that presencing presences. The opening grants first of all the possibility of the path to presence, and grants the possible presencing of that presence itself. (Heidegger, *Basic Writings* 55)

In his analysis of the fragments of Anaximander, Heraclitus, and Parmenides, Heidegger attempts to "retrieve" the lost sense of *einai* as presencing, a sense masked by the very structure of our language. Inherently, language is not an external, propositional, representation of an immediately given present. Neither is it a means by which the mind comes into contact with a transcendental signified. There is no ontological gap, nor two separate realms of existence, one mapped onto the other. For Heidegger, as Cornay has noted, language becomes the site for the "self-emerging and self-unfolding power of life and at the same time the excluded supplement of Greek *"einai"* comes to presence" (39). The excluded supplement is the movement from absence to presence and it is precisely this movement that is lost in propositional discourse which would bring being to a stand.

According to Heidegger, the Greeks were the first people to experience entities as *"phainomena"*—as things that of themselves show themselves or appear (see Heidegger's "On the Being and Conception of *Physis* in Aritstole's Physics"). *Phainesthai* means that an entity brings itself to self-manifestation (*sich zum Schienen bringen*) and "is," precisely insofar as it shows itself in that self-manifestation. Heidegger maintains that the Greeks, especially Aristotle, read entities as *"phainomena"* which show up in a field of meaningful presence: "as-ness" or "is-ness," as such.

It is such a question that is responsible for one of the more problematic concerns of Western ontology: the relation of beings and being, sensibles and ideas, the many and the one. It was such a concern that led Socrates to the conclusion (at least in one reading) that the world of ideas can exist separately from the sensible world. Given that "interminable flux" is intolerable, a realm of stability has to be posited, a realm open to definition and classification. But if one maintains such a strong separation between two distinct ontological realms, there arises the problem of how to relate the two. Some coherent notion of this relation must be explicated and substantiated.

The philosophical consequences of this problematic forces one to radically scrutinize statements of the form "x is," "x is identical with x," "x is different from y," "x is y," and so on. But it may be the case that merely tidying up a set of inadequate logical axioms, so as to provide a reformed logic of the nature of being, is insufficient. Heidegger writes,

> Being as the element of thinking, is abandoned by the technical interpretation of thinking. 'Logic,' beginning with the Sophists and Plato, sanctions this explanation. Thinking is judged by a standard that does not measure up to it. Such judgment may be compared to the procedure of trying to evaluate the nature and powers of a fish by seeing how it can live on dry land (*Basic Writings* 195).

From the standpoint of technical thinking both being and thought are narrowed and thereby violated, as the rigidity of logical categories precludes the possibility of expressing the nature of being, which always overflows the constraints of such categorical imposition. The notion that our thoughts and propositions must be "fixed" by corresponding to the "real," if they are to be significant, is a result of a desire to know and contain being as well as a result of construing being as a whole, present entity. Only if being is contained in this manner can we be sure of our representations, can we have certainty.

Heidegger has argued that "the transformation of Being to certainty stems from the criterion of 'whatness'":

> In the essential change of truth as veritas to certitudo, Being is prefigured as the representedness of self-representing in which the essence of subiecity develops. The simplest name for the determination of the beingness of beings in preparation here is the will, will as willing-itself. . . . The essential fullness of the will cannot be determined with respect to the will as a faculty of the soul. The will must rather be brought to essential unity with appearance: 'idea,' 're-praesentio,' 'becoming evident,' 'portraying itself,' 'attaining itself,' 'transcending itself,'

and thus 'having itself,' and thus 'being.' [*End of Philosophy* 57]

This desire for certainty, the positing of truth as the "distinctive trait of the intellect," in terms of knowing and representation, marks for Heidegger the inception of modern metaphysics.

> If the essence of truth, having become certainty, brings about its adequate relation to what is real through and for man who is placed in the essence of truth by requiring him to construct what is knowable as that which can be produced with certainty; and if the certainty of this construction requires that basis in which certainty's own essence is incorporated as the foundation, then something real must be secured in advance for all representational thinking. . . . [26]

In Descartes' philosophy, rational consciousness, consciousness as representation becomes, in the Cartesian meditations, the guarantor of certainty and knowledge: "something true is that which man of himself clearly and distinctly brings before himself and confronts as what is thus brought before him (re-presented) in order to guarantee what is represented in such a confrontation" (25). The assurance of such a representation is certainty. What is true in the sense of being certain is what is real. Thus, Descartes will argue: "our inquiries should be directed, not to what others have thought, nor to what we ourselves conjecture, but to what we can clearly and perspicuously behold and with certainty deduce . . ." (Rule 3) and "if a man observe them [the rules] accurately, he shall never assume what is false as true, and will never spend his mortal efforts to no purpose" ("Rules for the Direction of the Mind"). Reality becomes that which is open to the mind's act or re-presenting. In this way then, the split between subject and object is generated. Representational thinking brings about the presentation of the opposition of the object. This objectivity becomes, as Heidegger points out, systematized. With the dawn of the Enlightenment "true" knowledge becomes the privilege of the pure attentive intelligence. As Foucault has put it,

Resemblance, which had for long been the fundamental category of knowledge: both form and the content of what we know: became dissociated in an analysis based on terms of identity and difference; moreover, whether indirectly by the intermediary of measurement, or directly and, as it were, on the same footing, comparison became a function of order; and lastly, comparison ceased to fulfill the function of revealing how the world is ordered, since it was now accomplished according to the order laid down by thought. . . . (*Order of Things* 54)

The mind becomes engaged in the discursive task of differentiation, discrimination and the establishment of identities. By the distinct representation of things and the clear comprehension of the connection between things, certainty is assured. Concomitantly, language is no longer seen as "one of the figurations of the world" (Foucault 56). The task of language is now set in terms of representation: of the truth of things: "language has withdrawn from the midst of beings themselves and has entered a period of transparency and neutrality" (56). Foucault elicits two moments which are indicative of the "age of reason":

1) The inception of a theoretical model which is applied certain fields of knowledge.

2) The attempt to mathematicize empirical knowledge: (mathesis as a universal science of measurement and order).

Thus, relations between beings are to be conceived in the form of order and measurement: the method of "analysis" becomes paramount. However, Foucault is quick to point out that this mathesis does not entail that all knowledge is reduced to algebraic formulations. Rather, the "science of order" gives rise to a host of empirical disciplines: general grammar, natural history, the analysis of wealth, and so forth. These disciplines were situated respectively within the domain of words, beings, and needs. They were dependent then, not on the algebraic method but the "system of signs."

> This relation to Order is as essential to the Classical age as the relation to interpretation was to the Renaissance. And just as interpretation in the sixteenth century, with its superimposition of a semiology upon a hermeneutics, was essentially a knowledge based upon similitude, so the ordering of things by means of signs constitutes all empirical forms of knowledge as knowledge based upon identity and difference. (57)

This ordering and differentiation becomes indicative of the role that signs adopt in the post-Classical age, an age which sees the rise of science and technology. It is no longer the case that there can be an "unknown" sign (59), the meaning of which was to be discovered. This is not because we have discovered all possible signs but because "there can be no sign until there exists a *known* possibility of substitution between two known elements. The sign does not wait in silence for the coming of a man capable of recognizing it; it can be constituted only by an act of knowing" (59). Thus the sign is both constituted by and used by the knowing process. Even within the logical positivism of our own century the legacy of this transformation of the sign is evident. It was the sign system, as Foucault argues, that connects all knowledge to a language, and then replaces all languages with a system of artificial symbols and operations of a logical nature (predicate calculus would be an appropriate example). Thus, language is completely confined to its representational role.

Given this grammatical narrowing of the scope of language, in terms of a re-presentation of a fully present "being," temporality as the movement of revealing / concealing is entirely lost to thought. It is Heidegger's project to "retrieve" that lost sense of *einai*, through a "destruction," a step back, into the tradition. Given that in the next chapter we will be considering Heidegger's attempt to circumvent the restriction of the grammatical structure of metaphysical discourse, I would like to consider briefly, the way in which Heidegger attempts to re-evaluate the nature of *logos*. Despite the fact that some scholars may be "unhappy" at Heidegger's "mis-reading" of Aristotle (bearing in mind that the univocity of meaning is made problematical in this study), the discussion of *kinesis* was, on Heidegger's own admission, a motivating force for his subsequent discussion of the relation between being and time.

As Thomas Sheehan has argued, Heidegger sees *logos* as a modality of that which Aristotle called *energeia ateles*, construed as the incomplete appearance of beingness. *Physis* is inherently conjoined to *kinesis*. Heidegger's term *Eignung*, the "appropriation," relates to the possibility of the appearance of a natural entity, the entity is in a state of "becoming," of "being-underway" (*Unterwegesein*), where the operative principle is the movement of disclosure. We must now examine what constitutes this disclosure. We noted above that entities appear within a field of meaningful presence: "as" something. This "as-dimension" is related to human "essence" as *aletheuein*, disclosure. It is humans who raise the question of what being is as being, and thus any subsequent ontological speculation is at the same time phenomenological. Humans have access to entities only in terms of the latter's presence in *logos* and it is through the disclosive power of *logos* that the "is-ness" of entities becomes manifest, whether as "idea" or as "substance."

> In its essence language is not the utterance of an organism; nor is it the expression of a living thing. Nor can it ever be thought in an essentially correct way in terms of its syntactic character, perhaps not even in terms of the character of signification. Language is the lightening-concealing advent of Being itself. (*Basic Writings* 206)

So far the discussion has only concerned *physei on* or natural entities, that is a particular region of being. An obvious question is whether the unity of all modes of being of all regions of entities may not itself be this originary movement from absence to presence. Although for Heidegger, Aristotle's notion of *physis* marks a "regional narrowing" of the notion of being, he still conceives the *Physics* as inherently a metaphysical treatise, inasmuch as it inquires into the beingness (*ousia*) of a particular group of entities. Heidegger focuses on two key ideas: that *physis* is a kind of beingness, and thus the inquiry into *physis* is an ontolgical one, and secondly, and perhaps most importantly, the characterization of *physis* as *kinesis*: *ta physei (onta) kinoumena einai* (Aristotle, *Physics* A, 2, 185a, 12ff). Thus, Heidegger discerns *kinesis* as a kind of beingness. It is this determination of the nature of *kinesis* that becomes the basis for the understanding of both Aristotle's and the pre-Socratics' construal of *physis*. It was not that Aristotle was the first to raise the question concerning the essence of *kinesis*, but for Heidegger he elevated movement to a new level of questioning by grasping it as a mode of being, not just as the movement of entities but as their state of being moved. Thus, to designate *kinesis*, Heidegger uses the term *Bewegeit*, in the sense of *Bewegtstein*: "movedness" or "being-moved."

How then is *kinesis* to be construed ontologically, and further, in what way does this characterization lead to and effect the ontological determination of *physis*. The major part of Heidegger's commentary on Aristotle's work concerns the attempt to demonstrate that Aristotle reads *physis* in terms of *kinesis* and, therefore, the essence of *physis* is characterized by the unity of absence and presence. We may want to ask at this point, what is the function of *logos* in this scheme? *Logos* appears as a field in which a moving entity is temporarily brought to a stand or captured for a while, as it were. An entity inasmuch as it is in a process of generation is in a state of presence / absence. *Physis*, construed in this way, remains a continual source for the possibility of the appearance of entities: an ever repeatable presence / absence. Absence then becomes the very condition for the presentness of entities. This emphasis on movement (in terms of absence / presence) seriously undermines the metaphysical conception of being, as a whole, present totality. Similarly, being necessarily overflows the static representations of the "knowing " mind. If the "modern age" has given privilege to representation over resemblance, as Foucault has argued, it has equally privileged the subject *qua* rational consciousness as the primary locus for the disclosure of being. It is to the centrality of the knowing subject to which I shall now turn.

2. The Being of The Subject

The role of rational consciousness in modern metaphysics leads to the positing of the subject at the center of the disclosure of being. But it is not clear that we can assume such a consciousness as "given." Nietzsche has done much to demonstrate (albeit somewhat cryptically at times) that the epistemological primacy of rational consciousness is as much dependent upon a certain interpretation of subjectivity as "being *qua* presence" is dependent upon a particular interpretation of being.

For Nietzsche, the truth of being as represented by Western ontology is "A mobile army of metaphors, metonymies, anthropomorphisms . . . truths are illusions of which one has forgotten that they are illusions" ("On Truth and Falsity in their Ultramoral Sense," *Complete Works* 2: 180). To know being is to have power over the world. The interminable flux, the chaos, must be ordered. As Gayatri Spivak has noted in her "Preface" to *Of Grammatology* (xxii), as early as 1873 Nietzsche described metaphor as the originary process of what the intellect presents as truth: "The intellect, as a means for the preservation of the individual, develops its chief power in dissimulation" ("On Truth and Falsity" 174). As Derrida writes, "Nietzsche provides an entire thematics of active interpretations, which substitutes an incessant deciphering of 'reality' for the disclosure of truth as presentation of the thing itself" (*Speech and Phenomena* 149).

The metaphysical notion of the "subject" is also an interpretation (of human being as subject of interpretation) and never a "given": "it is a superadded invention, stuck onto the tail" (*Will to Power* 267). For Nietzsche, "knowledge" is a chimera, a dream that the philosopher acquiesces to. It is a refusal to accept that our knowledge, our history, are interpretations and not anchored in any absolute foundation, be it mind or God:

> How far the perspective character of existence extends or indeed whether existence has any other character than this; whether existence without 'sense,' does not become 'nonsense'; whether, on the other hand, all existence is not essentially an interpreting existence: that cannot be decided even by the most industrious and most scrupulously conscientious analysis and self-examination of the intellect; for in the course of this analysis the human intellect cannot avoid seeing in its own perspective forms, and only in these. We cannot look around our own corner.
> (*Gay Science* 336)

The dismissal of the subject as point of origin of truth also implies the dismissal of its opposite: the objective. Being is no *given*. In fact the whole notion of opposites is itself a construction: "There are no opposites: only from those [categories] of logic do we derive the concept of opposites: and falsely translate it to things" (*Will to Power* 298).

Enlightenment oppositions between metaphor and concept, the fictive and the real, are dissolved in Nietzsche. In a way somewhat different form Heidegger, Nietzsche affirms an active forgetfulness rather than a "retrieval" of that which has been forgotten: "It is not enough that you understand in what ignorance man and beast live; you must also have and acquire the *will* to ignorance" (328). By flying in the face of wisdom (wisdom for Nietzsche is merely a form of the will to power), play and the joy of risk-taking are affirmed.

> Wisdom: that seems to the rabble to be a kind of flight, an artifice and means for getting oneself out of a dangerous game; but the genuine philosopher: as he seems to us, my friends: lives 'unphilosophically' and 'unwisely', above all *imprudently* . . . he *risks* himself constantly, he plays the dangerous game. (*Beyond Good and Evil* 113)

It is the interpretive act, which, as Spivak points out, allows for the bypassing of metaphysical security ("Preface" xxx).

Although, unlike Heidegger, the *Übermensch* will "dance" outside of the "house of being," and there will be no nostalgic search for the truth of being, the Nietzschean insistence on the inherently narrowing effect of logocentric discourse is taken up by Heidegger in such works as *On The Way To Language*, where the dialogue with the Japanese scholar addresses the problem of thinking outside of metaphysical categories and stresses the need to embark upon such a task. Heidegger's new experience with language, as we shall see later, is an attempt to circumvent the restrictions of metaphysical determination.

The Heideggerian retrieval of metaphysics turns on a realization of the finitude of modes of disclosure and the finitude of the subject. It is the dual notions of finitude and historicity that primarily concern Heidegger's treatment of *Dasein* in *Being and Time*. Like Nietzsche, Heidegger is aware that our determinations of what constitutes subjectivity are interpretations and not discoveries. Such a posture is diametrically opposed to that of traditional ontology which, in attempting to know being in totality also aims at defining the essential nature of human beings. The "what am I" question is a corollary to the being-question. The quest for man's essence relies on the same metaphysical presuppositions as the search for the intrinsic nature of being.

In *Letter On Humanism*, Heidegger asks whether man's essence can be thought from the presupposition that man is marked off from other creatures. Perhaps we will be able to state correct predicates that obtain only and exclusively to human being but do we thereby locate what is essential to human beings? Heidegger believes that

> . . . we must be clear on this point, that when we do this we abandon man to the essential realm of *animalitas* even if we do not equate him with beasts but attribute a specific difference to him. In principle we are still thinking of *homo animalis*: even when *anima* (soul) is posited as *animus sive*

> *mens* (spirit or mind), and this in turn is later posited as
> subject, person, spirit *(Geist)*. *(Basic Writings* 203)

As we saw above, the metaphysical posture desires to represent its
object, and thus human being is equally represented with an
essence posited *a priori*. But Heidegger insists that this is merely
to remain at the level of "animalitas" and does not think in the
direction of "humanitas." Man, from the perspective of
metaphysics, appears as a complicated machine, subject to
analysis and control. But this is to overlook a fundamental point.
What has been forgotten is the fact that such analyses rely on
human being's first having a world and a language to articulate
that world and him/herself. Such standing in the "light of being"
(204) Heidegger calls "ek-sistence": the "ek-sistence" of man. "Ek-
sistence" becomes the possibility of reason and all discursive
practice:

> The human body is something essentially other than an
> animal organism. Nor is the error of biologism overcome
> by adjoining a soul to the human body, a mind to the soul,
> and the existential to the mind, and then louder than before
> singing the praises of the mind: only to let everything
> relapse into 'life-experience,' with a warning that thinking
> by its inflexible concepts disrupts the flow of life and that
> thought of Being distorts existence. (204)

Human being's essence, like that of being, cannot be
captured by technical mastery; it slips away. To ask the who? or
what? of man is already to have missed the point; it is to fall back
into the metaphysical search for an object: be it primarily rational
or animal. Heidegger speaks of ek-sistence in a way that must be
distinguished from the way the metaphysician speaks of
"existence": "the ecstatic essence of man consists in ek-sistence,
which is different from the metaphysically conceived *existentia*"
(205). This is neither the medieval *actualitas* nor the Kantian
objectivity of experience. Ecstatic (from the Greek *ekstasis*) means
the way man "stands out" in the truth of being. Deciding in what

manner man stands out will be our concern in the next chapter, where we will examine *Dasein's* being-in-the-world as an attempt to disrupt metaphysical notions of the human subject that would deny the inherent worldliness and temporal nature of the self. For now, however, I would like to digress briefly to consider a problem which ineluctably confronts my task in this study.

3. Moral Language

It might be thought that in critiquing the metaphysics of presence I have in someway precluded the possibility of deploying such a notion as "responsibility," inasmuch as this term is thoroughly embedded within traditional ethical categories: obligations, rights, duties, etc. Given, as I have suggested above, that we must be able to use and erase our language at one and the same time, it could be argued that this is precisely the move to make with respect to "moral language." It will, I hope, become evident by the end of this study, that my use of the notion of "responsibility" is not contained within the parameters of that binary opposition operating between rights and duties; in fact, my deployment of the term is not contained by reference to any logocentric categories. Just as the Derridean terms that we shall be encountering always signify more than logocentrism would allow, so does "responsibility."

To demonstrate that I am not flippantly disregarding the objection, I will conclude this chapter by insisting that there is a distinction to be drawn between "morality" and the larger class of evaluative terms. What are the specific features of morality which distinguish it from other modes of evaluation and make it essentially ideological? From the standpoint of the tradition (at least pre-Hegelian), morality is premised on the assumption of "individual" responsibility. Inherent in this view is the assumption that obligations and rights accrue primarily to autonomous agents. Already in place is the belief that subjects are externally rather than internally related. Furthermore, morality is defined by its alienated character; it is typically expressed as a set of external requirements to which the individual must conform.

The motivation for the "responsibility" that I will discuss will not be concerned with imperatives—the imposition of moral commands. I will not be speaking of a notion of responsibility that is generated by a code or system but as a mode of "responding" which flows directly out of the respect of difference. Heidegger has spoken of "Gelassenheit" ("Letting-be"); "responsibility" as a responding to the other is also a "letting be" without the desire either to control, marginalize, or exclude the other. This theme will be developed in greater detail in the final chapter. For now it is important simply to recognize that the term "responsibility" need not be understood within, or confined to, the traditional context of individual responsibility, rights, and duties.

It is significant and, indeed, interesting to note the way the *mode d'assujettissement* (mode of obligation) changes as we enter different historical epochs. Foucault writes:

> . . . nobody is obliged in classical ethics to behave in such a way as to be truthful to their wives, to not touch boys, and so on. But if they want to have a beautiful existence, if they want to have a good reputation, if they want to be able to rule others, they have to do that. ("Genealogy of Ethics" 356)

However, when we reach the Stoic period, this personal choice aspect ceases to be the primary motivation; now, as Foucault continues, "you have to do it because you are a rational being." The mode of obligation is changing. With the inception of Christianity, religious institutions become the framework for ethical norms. It is the juridical aspect of religious law that is maintained when religion stops being the motivating factor. Thus when we arrive at the Enlightenment:

> . . . the religious framework of those rules disappears in part, and then between a medical or scientific approach and a juridical framework there was competition, with no resolution. (357)

We shall be considering in "The Self and Power" (Part Two) the varieties of normalizing strategies operative in post-Enlightenment society, but for now it is enough to stress the fact that ethical modes of obligation are subject to radical, historical change. But there appears to be a common element in Stoic and Christian modes: asceticism. The type of self-creation indicative of these ethical postures entails the act of "knowing" oneself and "knowing" the "truth."

> Even if it is true that Greek philosophy founded rationality, it always held that a subject could not have access to truth if he did not first operate upon himself a certain work which would make him susceptible to knowing the truth: a work of purification, conversion of the soul by contemplation of the soul itself. (371)

The Enlightenment constitutes a rupture, a break from this tradition. The Cartesian insistence that "To accede to truth, it suffices that I be *any* subject which can see what is evident" (cited by Foucault 371) leads inevitably to a "nonascetic" subject of knowledge. The "science of knowing" can proceed unfettered by self analysis.

Of course, there were attempts to ameliorate the dichotomy. As Foucault notes,

> There was much debate in the Enlightenment as to whether these subjects were completely different or not. Kant's solution was to find a universal subject, which, to the extent that it was universal, could be the subject of knowledge, but which demanded nonetheless, an ethical attitude: precisely the relationship to the self which Kant proposes in *The Critique of Practical Reason*. (372)

Thus, Kant reintroduces ethics, from its Cartesian exile. Descartes had driven a wedge between ethics and scientific rationality; Kant brings the two together again by a from of what Dreyfus and Rabinow term "procedural rationality" (*Foucault*

Reader 372). Ethics becomes the conformity of the self to "practical reason." As a universal subject I must obey the commands of a universal moral law. But the fusion of ethics and rationality is deceptive. What we are dealing with, I believe, is the subsumption of ethics under rationality. It is the latter term that dominates. Given that I have argued thus far that rationalism is precisely the force that has generated our current global predicament, it is our task to free ethics from rationalism. How this is to be accomplished is the task of this present study.

While I do not intend to unduly valorize the Greek ethical experience, certain features of this experience seem to have been neglected in post-Enlightenment thinking which, if resurrected, may serve our task of freeing the ethical subject from the totalizing effects of rationalism. In his discussion of the moral problematization of pleasures in Greek society, Foucault argues that:

> The principle according to which this activity [sexual] was meant to be regulated, the 'mode of subjection,' was not defined by a universal legislation determining permitted and forbidden acts, but rather by a *savoir-faire*, an art that prescribed the modalities of a use that depended on different variables (need, time, status). (*Use of Pleasure* 91).

What had to be effected was an "aesthetics of existence" in which one constituted oneself as an ethical subject. Foucault suggests that "classical antiquity's moral reflection concerning the pleasures was not directed toward a codification of acts, nor toward a hermeneutics of the subject, but toward a stylization of attitudes and an aesthetics of existence" (92). Thus, we are concerned with a stylistics of the subject in which the self is fashioned and not discovered. Furthermore, the successful accomplishment of this aesthetics of existence could not be achieved separately from praxis. Such a posture is markedly distinct from the universal and abstract self of post-Enlightenment thought.

> The time would come when the art of the self would
> assume its own shape, distinct from the ethical conduct
> that was its objective. But in classical Greek thought, the
> 'ascetics' that enabled one to make oneself into an ethical
> subject was an integral part: down to its very form: of the
> practice of a virtuous life, which was also the life of a 'free'
> man in the full, positive and political sense of the word.
> (77)

The important point to recognize, is that the moral
requirements that were implied by "the constitution of this self-
disciplined subject were not presented in the form of a universal
law, which each and every individual would have to obey" (77).
The "ought" aspect is missing. I perform virtuous acts so as to give
my existence "the most graceful and accomplished form possible"
(251).

This brief example is useful from our perspective inasmuch
as it demonstrates that we can formulate an ethics without
recourse to universal moral principles or divine edicts, binding
upon all. It introduces a certain flexibility and perhaps evokes a
pluralistic and innovative approach to how we constitute
ourselves as subjects. K. J. Dover has remarked that:

> The Greeks neither inherited nor developed a belief that a
> divine power had revealed to mankind a code of laws for the
> regulation of sexual behavior; they had no religious
> institution possessed of the authority to enforce sexual
> prohibitions. Confronted by cultures older and richer and
> more elaborate than theirs, cultures which nonetheless
> differed greatly from each other, the Greeks felt free to
> select, adopt, develop and, above all, innovate. (252)

Innovation in the field of ethics relies in part upon our readiness
to dispute the post-Enlightenment belief that the moral subject is
constituted entirely within the parameters of reason. As Reiner
Schurmannn has recently remarked, Foucault's genealogies can
effect a transformation in the way we constitute ourselves as

ethical subjects (a lecture at the Eastern Division of the American Philosophical Association). They thematize the subject's insertion into an epochal order. Such "epochal topographies" or *exposés* provide us with points of discursive interventions in those areas where particular power configurations release effects of subjection and control. We will consider precisely how the genealogical method generates this intervention in Part Two.

So far we have attempted to show the way in which the metaphysical construal of being, as presence, gives rise to an essentialist conception of the self. The decisive turn which constitutes modern metaphysics is the positing of truth as the distinctive trait of the intellect. From this point of view, the rational subject becomes the locus and site of disclosure of being, and knowledge becomes the privilege of the pure attentive intelligence. We have further seen that by way of a "retrieval" of the tradition Heidegger brings to light a fundamental lack within metaphysical thought: the forgetfulness of the inherent temporality of being. From a parallel perspective, we have argued that the constitution of the subject indicative of Western rationalism relies on the same metaphysical presuppositions as the constitution of being. Both Heidegger and Nietzsche recognize the necessity of overcoming the decidedly narrowing effect of the metaphysical categories whether they are imposed upon the "real" or the self. We will now again take up the discussion of the self by examining in greater detail Heidegger's attempt to situate the subject with reference to its concernful being-in-the-world and its temporality.

From *Dasein* to *Ereignis*

1. Heidegger's Existential Analytic of *Dasein*

> *Dasein* does not have the kind of Being which belongs to
> something merely present-at-hand within the world, nor
> does it ever have it. So neither is it to be presented
> thematically as something we come across in the same way
> as we come across what is present-at-hand. (*Being and
> Time* s. 9)

The primary deficiency of traditional ontology, for
Heidegger, is that it attempts an analysis of the entities disclosed
to people without undertaking a serious examination of the being
of *Dasein*. One particular, traditional interpretation of the
encounter between *Dasein* and things assumes precedence, that of
man as the detached observer. The goal of fundamental ontology is
to render a more complete account of the structures that
constitute *Dasein*'s being-in-the-world. Although *Dasein* shares
the characteristics of being-*in*-the world with other entities, it is
more than merely another thing as only to *Dasein* can things be
revealed. Thus, it is constituted as the *there* of being, the place or
site of disclosure. We must stress, however, that the spectatorial
stance, the perspective of the detached observer, is only one mode
in which beings are related to *Dasein* and a derivative one at that.
Heidegger attempts to circumvent the narrowing of *Dasein*'s
worldliness, effected by such a posture by suggesting that "we
choose a way of access and such a kind of interpretation that this

entity can show itself and form itself. And this means that it is to be shown as it is 'proximally' and for the most part, in its everydayness" (s. 16, 17).

The traditional insistence that we first encounter the things around us as objects, facts, is radically misconceived. Our understanding of our world is thoroughly dependent on and interrelated to our aims and concerns. As Heidegger says: "*Dasein*, when understood *ontologically* is care. Because Being-in-the-world belongs essentially to *Dasein*: its Being towards the world (*Sein zur Welt*) is essentially concern" (s. 12). Our common everyday exposure to entities is experienced in terms of their use; the scientific posture of detached observation is secondary. To cite an example of Karsten Harries in her "Fundamental Ontology and the Search of Man's Place," if one is to ask what is the true essence of the tree blooming in the yard, one would need, from the standpoint of traditional ontology, to strip off any possible subjectivist interpretation (perhaps that of the artist, farmer, etc.) constituted by different individuals. Only by a thorough decontextualization can the real tree be disclosed (70). Precisely this type of reductionist ontology, Heidegger refuses to countenance. Further, it might be noted that along with this anti-reductionist approach the age old problems of the status of things disappears. There is no need to ponder interminably upon how the self managed to "break its isolation" (70) and come into contact with entities outside. This is only a problem for the devotee of the "detached observer" camp. "The 'scandal of philosophy' [that there is no proof of an external world] is not that this proof has yet to be given, but that such proofs are expected and attempted again and again" (Heidegger, *Being and Time* s. 205). Being-in-the-world is constitutive of *Dasein's* existence and in no way peripheral to it. *Dasein* cannot choose to be unconcerned with its world, all detachment is at once a pure abstraction. In a similar fashion, being-with-others is constitutive of *Dasein's* existence. "So far as *Dasein is* at all, it has Being-with-another as its kind of Being" (s. 125).

While the first part of Heidegger's analytic of *Dasein* concerns its everydayness, a mode of being more fundamental than that disclosed by science, it is not enough merely to state the various modes of being indicative of *Dasein's* factical existence, as if *Dasein* were merely an entity amongst other entities—a thing among things. For Heidegger, "there-being" is no subject, but transcendence (Richardson, "Heidegger's Way through Phenomenology" 88)—the site of the disclosure of being. But this transcendence should not be seen as a falling back upon the primacy of consciousness. As Richardson concludes,

> As to-be-in-the-world, then, There-being is not opposed to the world as a subject opposed to an object but is simply the luminosity of the World / Being because it is the coming-to-pass of truth. With such a conception, the entire Idealism / Realism problematic, and with it such things as the critical problem, dissolves. (88)

There is no longer the problem of eliciting the relation between self and world as if they were externally related. What needs to be stressed is that ontologically *Dasein* is the site of this coming-to-pass of the truth of being. Given that *Dasein's* "ownmost possibility" is its being-toward-death, it is precisely finitude and negativity that marks being. Both *Dasein* and being, are "processes," and as Richardson points out, "the process is temporo-historical" (88). It is this fundamental insight that remains hidden from the perspective of traditional ontology.

Although incapable of being free from immersion in the projects of everyday life, *Dasein* must develop the resolve to step from its everyday existence, its ontic facticity. But such a resolve inevitably begins with a certain anxiety, a loss of place and a loss of security. Of course one can readily immerse oneself in the concerns of the "they" or refuse to look resolutely into the abyss; one may also withdraw into the silence (this is perhaps the Wittgensteinian option), but perhaps there is a third option which does not result either in isolated contemplation or forgetfulness but in a radical praxis.

> Resoluteness, as authentic Being-one's-Self, does not detach
> *Dasein* from its world, nor does it isolate it so that it
> becomes a free-floating 'I.' And how would it when
> Resoluteness as authentic disclosedness, is authentically
> nothing else than Being-in-the-World? Resoluteness brings
> the Self right into its concernful being: alongside what is
> ready-to-hand, pushes it into solicitous Being-with-
> Others. (Heidegger, *Being and Time* s. 298)

Isolation and detachment then are not merely ineffective remedies
but an ontological impossibility. *Dasein* cannot choose to be non-
worldly but it does have the capacity to understand that
worldedness and the finitude of the particular modes of being that
constitute it. The "authentic" step-back into the tradition, allows
Dasein to distance itself from its everyday concern in an attempt
to recognize the historical situatedness of all modes of disclosure.

There has been a tendency I think, on the part of some
commentators—for instance Paul Ricoeur in "Heidegger and the
Question of the Subject"—to collapse the distinction between the
inherently anthropomorphic analysis of the belonging together of
being and man in *Being and Time* and the insistence, in the later
writings, of the primordiality of the relation holding between
being, time, and language. It has been argued, that from
Heidegger's critique of metaphysical notions of subjectivity (i.e.
the "destruction" of the Cartesian *cogito*), one might be able to
retain at least the centrality of the "I"—albeit in a different guise.
Can, then, anything be gained from holding on to some
notion of the "I"? Obviously not in terms of privileging the "I
think." However, what of the "I am"? Ricoeur's aim in
"Heidegger and the Question of the Subject," is both to accept
Heidegger's refusal of the Cartesian *cogito* (at least if it is
conceived as a "simple epistemological principle") yet preserve
the efficacy of the "I am" and the "ontological purpose which was
in the *cogito* and which has been forgotten in the formulation of
Descartes" (224). It is clear that while Ricoeur wishes to embrace
the Heideggerian critique of the Cartesian *cogito*, he does believe

that a rejuvenated and existentialized "I" will be of service for an adequate understanding of being and for demonstrating the connection between Heidegger's early and late writing. Ricoeur sees the shift of emphasis between the analytic of *Dasein* and Heidegger's philosophy of language as manifesting the same problematic but under a different guise: "the rise of *Dasein* as self and the rise of language as speech or discourse (*parole*) are one and the same problem" (224).

The crucial fact, for him, seems to be that the question of the meaning of being is determined by that which the question is about. Thus, a reduction to the epistemic priority of *Dasein*, as point of origin of the inquiry would do violence to the matter at hand. But Ricoeur argues "at the same time we discover the possibility of a new philosophy of the ego in the sense that the genuine ego is constituted by the question itself" (226). Although traditional ontology, in giving priority to the ego enters into a forgetfulness of the question as question, Ricoeur believes that such a perspective opens up a twofold relation which he is concerned to analyze. How is the self implicated? It cannot be in terms of the "I think," but some entity is implied in the question, the "I am." Thus, we have the privileging of the existential over the epistemic construal of the *cogito*. It is here that I must insist, *contra* Ricoeur, that I do not read Heidegger's later writings as a reinstatement of the *cogito* on ontological grounds (as perhaps would be justified in reading *Being and Time*). The retrieval of the Cartesian *cogito* and the centrality of Dasein becomes significantly undermined once the "new" experience with language is attempted. It is not the "think" in the "I think," nor the "am" in the "I am" that is problematic, but the "I"—it is the "I" that is displaced and transfigured.

However, Ricoeur is aware that the primacy of the *cogito* is in fact dependent upon a particular time and place. In quoting from Heidegger's *Die Zeit des Weltbildes* (1938), he writes:

> the *cogito* is not an innocent assertion; it belongs to an age
> of metaphysics for which truth is the truth of existents and
> as such constitutes the forgetfulness of Being. (227)

Thus, the "philosophical ground on which the *cogito* emerged is the ground of science" (228). The *cogito* is "put at the disposal of an "explanatory representation'" (228). We have already seen the way in which Heidegger attempts to destruct the notion of the *cogito* as locus of truth. The critique of Cartesianism is precisely the undermining of the subject as spectator of the real and ground of the truth of representation. But, Ricoeur argues, Heidegger insists that this construal of the *cogito* was not that of the early Greeks. Thus, the destruction of the Cartesian *cogito* allows us to return to an earlier Greek notion of the ego, allows for a "repetition of the question of the ego" (Ricoeur 232). According to Ricoeur, we can then effect a bridge between the early and later writings of Heidegger by demonstrating the continuity of the philosophy of the self.

The reason that Ricoeur can argue for a retrieval of the *cogito* in the later writings is that he conceives Heidegger's writings on language as essentially depending on the fact that "the exegesis of *Dasein* must be replaced by an exegesis of the speech or discourse, the words, of the poet and thinker" (232). But what such an exegesis will show in Heidegger's hands is that the poet and the thinker respond to a call that issues from language. The poet is not privileged because he has somehow happened upon the "correct" code for the interpretation of being but because he has realized that such a code is impossible: "if man is to find his way once again into the nearness of Being he must first learn to exist in the nameless" (*Basic Writings* 199).

The similarities between the two inquiries (*Dasein* and language) could be maintained if one conceives language primarily as speech; the expression of and communication between self-present subjects. This might seem reasonable, perhaps, given that the self cannot fail to be implicated in the act of communication. But even if the word is the *Da* of *Dasein*, there need be no referral back to the *cogito* as individual site of disclosure. It could be argued that the problem of *Being and Time* was that it did conceive the *Da* anthropomorphically, and this limitation will not be resolved by an equally anthropomorphic construal of language. It further seems clear that in the later writings of Heidegger, if one remains at the level of speech and the speaking subject the *Da* can never be disclosed due to the incessant need to recuperate meaning, to communicate.

2. "Language Speaks Not Man"

Pervasive throughout all Heidegger's later writings is his insistence on the centrality of language, not merely as the discursive articulation of objects but more fundamentally as the site of *Dasein's* existence. Similarly, language becomes the central feature of the disclosure of being. This emphasis on language seriously disrupts the ontological presuppositions of traditional metaphysics. As Jacques Derrida points out, "All the names related to fundamentals, to principles, or to the center, have always designated an invariable presence: essence, existence, substance, subject, etc" (*Writing and Difference* 279-280). The inquiry into being *qua* being, as we saw in the last chapter, has traditionally been framed within the context of understanding being as a ground, which either accounts for or allows beings their presence. These inquiries have the unfortunate result of reducing being to a being. It is precisely for this reason that Heidegger uses the term *es gibt* (literally, it gives): "for 'is' is commonly said of something which is. We call such a thing a being. But Being 'is' precisely not 'a being'" (*Basic Writings* 214).

One of the consequences of what Heidegger has termed the "forgetfulness of being" is the misunderstanding of language, where its essence is taken to be self-expression and communication. What remains hidden is that language is the precondition both for expression (at least at any interesting level) and for subjectivity. We live so much under the domination of traditional metaphysical categories, that we are unable even to speak of being in a way appropriate to its inherent temporality, as the grammatical structure of our language is equally metaphysical.

Although language is the field of our experience and discourse, the medium through which the world becomes articulated, it is at one and the same time the limit of experience. As Nietzsche so aptly phrases it, "we are prisoners of our grammar" (*Will to Power* s. 522); we are confined to the articulation of our world via the dictates of a subject / predicate syntax. However, this realization is postponed, deferred, while we continue to understand knowledge from the standpoint of the self-contained subject as ego, which constitutes a paradigm example of such a structure. If the world is not self-articulating, if we do not merely discover neatly pre-packaged entities with their parameters clearly delineated and differentiated, then the discursive functioning of our cognitive apparatus appears as a "will to know" and a "will to order." Thus, Nietzsche will say, "not to know but to schematize" (s. 565). We are never directly acquainted with the "facts" of our world. Facticity is always a dyadic relation, involving selection and interpretation. Our attempt to critically examine our knowledge claims is thrown back to an attempt to elucidate our modes of knowing, to discover why we interpret the world as we do.

From the standpoint of the subject, linguistically constituted by the language of metaphysics, the world becomes radically anthropomorphized, reduced to the indubitability of the ego which projects its internal syntactic structure outwards toward the world. But Nietzsche asks: "Is not the incessant and unyielding imposition of this particular schema a fundamentally and finally destructive blunder?" (s. 550). In fact, in the moral sphere, our concern with "rational utility" is "precisely that fatal piece of stupidity from which we shall one day perish" (s. 550). Heidegger is also aware of the dangers inherent in reason's hegemony, as David Krell shows:

> . . . to insist that technology belongs to the destiny of the West in no way implies that it does not menace. On the contrary, the question concerning the essence of technology confronts supreme danger, which is that this one way of revealing beings many overwhelm man and

> beings and all other possible ways of revealing. Such danger
> is impacted in the essence of technology, which is an
> ordering of, or setting upon, both nature and man, a defiant
> challenging of beings that aims at total and exclusive
> mastery. The technological framework is inherently
> expansionist and can reveal only by reduction. Its attempt
> to enclose all beings in a particular claim (utter availability
> and sheer manipulability) Heidegger calls 'enframing.'
> ("Introduction" to *Basic Writings* 285)

Humanity is compelled to experience the consequences of an
uncritical allegiance to the dictates of rational disclosure.
Technology does more than merely provide us with the means of
subjugating the natural world; it inscribes our very thinking with
a desire to control, to subordinate. It is precisely here that the
danger lies. Yet, "where danger is, grows / The saving power also."
We cannot, however, take for granted Hölderlin's words. There is
a need for "preparation" and such preparation finds its basis in
questioning.

> Because the essence of technology is nothing technological,
> essential reflection upon technology and decisive con-
> frontation with it must happen in a realm that is, on the
> one hand, akin to the essence of technology and, on the
> other, fundamentally different from it. Such a realm is art.
> (*Basic Writings* 317)

What must be thought is that which allows the coming to pass of
technology; we must attempt to think the originary movement of
unconcealment.

For Heidegger, we need to turn to the poets rather than the
technocrat in our attempt to gesture to the "appropriating event"
or *Ereignis*. Perhaps to speak of being through poetic discourse is
the only way in which it may be spoken without narrowing the
notion in terms of logical categories, but the hearer must also be
able to respond to that which is heard. One must, says Heidegger
in "The Origin of the Work of Art," be open to the "call" of being

and "dwell" in light of that call. "Poetry is the saying of the unconcealedness of beings. Actual language at any given moment is the happening of this saying, which a people's world historically arises for it and the earth is preserved as that which remains closed" (*Basic Writings* 185).

There is an intimate connection between what Heidegger sees as the essence of art, that is, "all art is the letting happen of truth" (186) and the revelatory experience characterized by the aesthetic response. The "Conversation On A Country Path" is perhaps Heidegger's most poetic attempt to re-think being *as* time. We also notice in this work a shift in terminology. Being is now termed *die Gegnet* or "that-which-regions." The German word for "region" is *Gegend*, but as it is the "region of regions" (*die Gegend aller Gegend*) or the region that Heidegger is alluding to, he uses *die Gegnet*. As Anderson and Freund point out in a footnote to their translation of *Discourse on Thinking*, the use of the composite "that-which-regions," reflects a movement attributed by Heidegger to *die Gegnet* even though there is a tendency to reify the *that*, a tendency which however must be resisted.

The "Conversation" has its task the search for a thinking that is not a willing. The type of calculative thinking indicative of metaphysics and technology, the type of thinking that determines its object, must be overcome. We must, as Heidegger says "wean ourselves from will." The transition must be made from "willing" to "releasement," a task made more difficult since the releasement remains hidden.

> **Scientist:** In many respects it is clear to me what the word releasement should not signify for us. But at the same time, I know less and less what we are talking about. We are trying to determine the nature of thinking What has releasement to do with thinking? ("Conversation" 62)

The teacher replies to the scientist that his perplexity will not be resolved nor his question answered if thinking is construed in the traditional sense as representing. However, the nature of thinking that Heidegger is seeking may be "fixed in releasement."

Precisely how to speak about "releasement" is exceedingly problematic. Heidegger takes the risk, however, deploying the notion of "openness" as an aid. "**Teacher:** What is evident of the horizon then is but the side facing us of an openness which surrounds us; an openness which is filled with views of appearances of what to our re-presenting are objects" (64). The task becomes more difficult because "horizon" and "transcendence" are experienced only relative to objects and our representing them as such. What allows the horizon to be what it is has not yet been encountered. The horizon has a twofold character: it can manifest itself as the horizon of our representations as well as an openness. It is this openness that Heidegger calls a region, "an enchanted region where everything belonging there returns to that in which it rests" (65). We must still, however, discern how to speak of this region. As we noted earlier, the grammatical structure of our language, given its ontic character, is extremely ill-equipped to deal with this task, and Heidegger's attempt must be seen as a gesture, rather than a definitive statement. "**Teacher:** the region gathers just as if nothing were happening, each to each into an abiding" (66). Despite the verbal construction of "the region gathers," nothing is happening here; we are not concerned with an event in space-time as we are not concerned with an event of "appropriation." Heidegger goes on to couple the notion of "gathering" with that of waiting—although not a waiting *for* something:

> **Teacher:** In waiting we leave open what we are waiting for.
> **Scholar:** Why?
> **Teacher:** Because waiting releases itself into openness. . . .
> **Scholar:** . . . into the expanse of distance. . . .
> **Teacher:** . . . in whose nearness it finds the abiding in which it remains. (68)

Thus, as the scientist remarks, thinking would be "coming-into-the-nearness-of-distance." How then was this formulation arrived at? First there is the attempt, albeit possible only in a transitory way and of finite duration, to free oneself from all representational thinking. The course of the conversation then allows the scientist to "let himself into releasement as such." "**Teacher:** . . . releasement would be not only a path but a movement . . . which finds its rest in that-which-regions" (70). Openness and waiting are now brought together: "The relation to that-which-regions is waiting. And waiting means: to release oneself into the openness of that-which-regions" (72). This movement into *die Gegnet*, however, does not suggest that it is possible to stand outside "that-which-regions." As far as we think, our thinking (representation) stays within the transcendental horizon. But the horizon is only one side of *die Gegnet*, that side which is turned toward our thinking and our representing. "That-which-regions surrounds us and reveals itself to us as the horizon" (73). It is clear that we are not dealing with a subject but with the withdrawal of an event, as Theodore Kisiel has noted:

> . . . the apophantic language arrives at a predicate which bestows a definite character on a subject that already stands out, the hermeneutical language, groping in the most primordial pre-predicative realm, culminates in the 'saying that does not say' (*sagenden Nichtsagen*). In it, purely declarative sentences are no longer possible, its assertions take on a peculiarly non-assertive character, its propositions amount to a leap to which the usual logic of the substantive does not apply. ("The Language of the Event" 97)

It is precisely this new experience with language that is attempted in the "Conversation" that marks Heidegger's gesturing toward *Ereignis*.

Despite the fact that Heidegger is adamant in asserting that *Ereignis* is untranslatable, Kisiel suggests that we "bracket the teutonic pomposity of this declaration" (100). One might be able to explicate *Ereignis* in terms of the linguistic constellations used by Heidegger in his work. Rather than employ the use of neologisms, Heidegger prefers to "listen" attentively to the "archaic simplicity" of the "aboriginal language." What follows then is a "highly condensed linguistic analysis of Heidegger's most basic language in terms of the main linguistic constellations that thread through his conception of *Ereignis*" (101). First, we have the language of "coming and going" used to express the dynamics between man and being. *Ereignis* becomes the condition of possibility for this opposition in much the same way, as we shall see in the next chapter, that *différance* is thought as the possibility of all relation. However, *Ereignis* guides our thinking in the opposite direction also. As Kisiel notes, the second linguistic group consists of "stasis" words such as "standing," "bringing to stand," "posing," and "positing" (102). But most pervasively, it is "concealment" that Heidegger uses to gesture toward *Ereignis*, always remembering that concealing also gives rise to revealing, showing, *lassen*, and *Ereignis* becomes the dimension "enabling the emergence of beings."

However one construes *Ereignis*, one must be careful to avoid recourse to any term or constellation of terms that would somehow constitute a continuation of metaphysics and that appears to be inordinately difficult. We have seen, however, that despite the fact that questions of the type, "what is *Ereignis*?" are totally inappropriate, we might indulge in what André Schuwer in "Prolegomena to *Being and Time*" has called "preparational" thinking. In a way strikingly similar to Derrida's utilization of *différance*, Heidegger states in *The End of Philosophy* that "the task of this thinking which uses *Ereignis* as guide-word is very modest; it has the character of a preparation and not at all of a foundation. It suffices this kind of thinking to pro-voke the awakening of an availability of man for an outstanding and essential human possibility of which the contours remain obscure and of which the forthcoming remains unsure" (187). In a sense, as I shall be arguing in the final chapter, the attempt to "think" *Ereignis* is also to act—a particular type of comportment toward others. In a letter to Manfred Frings, Heidegger writes that

> thought can no longer, in terms of the traditional scheme of
> the distinction between theory and practice, be relegated to

the merely theoretical. One can experience thought as an original kind of acting (*Handeln*) that does not, indeed, aim at any immediate effects, but precisely for that reason surpasses in its very uselessness any type of technical-practical undertaking. In this way it prepares the determinability of the future existence of man. (cited in *Heidegger and the Path of Thinking* 187)

Schuwer points out that the type of acting envisaged by Heidegger is no intervention. There is no "intervening in the crisis of our civilization and thereby giving testimony to the tone and efficacy of thought," as with Ricoeur (188). According to Schuwer, what we have to do is "reach for the hand of being which is granted to us in *Ereignis* and which will give us (by willing not willing) time for the mystery of life and death, time for the earth in its splendor and expanding release, time for work which will not enslave, and perhaps time for God" (190).

Now, apart from sounding somewhat like a bad folk song, there seems to be something decidedly metaphysical about preserving time for this sort of contemplation. Perhaps this reading of Heidegger is over reverent or nostalgic (as Derrida would have it) about the mystery granted to us in *Ereignis*. Furthermore, this somewhat idyllic picture of serene contemplation is only a possibility for *certain Daseins*, and if our current political institutions are not significantly modified there will be no place for anything like contemplation or anything else for that matter. Heidegger is always insistent upon the fact that *Dasein* is not presented with the choice of whether or not to be concerned with its world. The detached observer, whether construed from the standpoint of the scientist or from the perspective of the mystic, is not an option. Inasmuch as the experience of *ereignis* reveals the finitude of all modes of disclosure, it cannot do other than provide a site of resistance to those ideological manifestations of metaphysics which would entrench particular *Gestells* as absolute and infinite. There seems to me to be ample evidence in Heidegger's remarks concerning technology to draw the inference that the experience of *Ereignis* reveals the transitory nature of that particular mode of enframing, the scientific world view. Given *Dasein's* concern with its world, there is no necessity that the experience of *Ereignis* manifest itself in silence and acquiescence; radical questioning is also an option, and one that I will be insisting on in the next chapter.

Whatever new social configurations may appear in a post-industrial world, they will, if they are to occur at all, be the result of the radical questioning or our present culture and our ethos. As Reiner Schurmann has argued,

> In a culture where philosophy has come to cooperate with the existing system to the point of radically abandoning its task of criticism, Heidegger insistence on releasement and 'life without why' as the practical *a priori* for the thought of Being opens an alternative way to think of life in society. (*Ontological Difference* 122)

In the next chapter I will deploy and examine a notion which can, I believe, be mapped onto or parallel *Ereignis*—a notion which both looks back to our discussion of *aletheia* in Chapter One, and which looks forward to our discussion of the self and power in Chapter Four; that notion is *différance*. However, as we shall see, with Derrida, there is no nostalgia, there is no desire to formulate a linguistic constellation adequate in pinning down the meaning of this elusive word, being. *Différance* is articulated precisely as the possibility of conceptuality and meaning.

Part Two

Displacing the Subject

Language, Structure, and Subject

1. Language and Difference

The major thrust of French Structuralism was to replace the subject by a system of structures, oppositions, and differences which, to be intelligible, need not be viewed as products of a living subjectivity at all. During the opening remarks on the nature of the linguistic sign, Ferdinand de Saussure makes the following statement:

> Our definition of the linguistic sign poses an important question of terminology. I call the combination of a concept and a sound-image a sign. . . . I propose to retain the word sign (*signe*) to designate the whole and to replace concept and sound-image respectively by signified (*signifié*) and signifier (*signifiant*), the last two terms have the advantage of indicating the opposition that separates them

from each other and from the whole of which they are parts. (*Course in General Linguistics* 67)

From this definition, two general laws or characteristics of the sign are possible. First, the joint association of the signified and the signifier in the sign necessitates that in use the linguistic sign is arbitrary. For example, Saussure notes that "the idea of 'sister' is not linked by any inner relationship to the succession of sounds s-ö-r which serves as its signifier in French, that it could be represented equally by just any other sequence is proved by differences among languages and by the very existence of different languages" (68).

However, it is important to note that the term "arbitrary" does not entail that the relationship holding between signifier and signified is left to the discretion of the individual speaker. Such an agent is not free to change a sign once it has been established in a linguistic community. Second, the nature of the signifier is linear in that it represents a single span that is measured in one dimension. That dimension is time, as Saussure points out: "In contrast to visual signifiers (nautical signals, etc.) which can offer simultaneous groupings in several dimensions, arbitrary signifiers have at their command only the dimension of time. Their elements are presented in succession; they form a chain" (70). Three questions become pertinent. In what sense is the sign a dyadic structure or, perhaps more precisely, how are we to construe the relationship between signifier and signified? What is the relationship holding between signification and meaning? What can be considered as the ontological status of language? An answer to the first two questions may shed some light on the third.

As we have noted, Saussure holds that signs are composed of signifiers and signifieds, sound-images and concepts. We must be careful of this picture if we are not to fall back into a variety of Lockean dualism. Although there is a certain tension evident in Saussure's position, I think he would agree that the signifier "represents" the signified, not according to an empirical association but rather the signifiers are a function, so to speak, of a single expression of the concepts (signifieds) that constitute the linguistic collectivity. Saussure believes that the faculty of articulating words is exercised only with the help of "the instrument created by the collectivity and provided for its use" (67). Language is not the function of the speaker. As with Wittgenstein, the sign is always a sign in use, a gesture, as Merleau-Ponty terms it. But just as the gesture is known within the context of its use, so the sign is known only through the context of other signs. The important point to grasp is that meaning as present in the signs is not signs themselves (as signifier and signified), but meaning *is* the signs. Inasmuch as a speaker uses meaningful sounds, this single instance of usage reflects the structure of a system. Thus, in speaking there is a paradigm that reflects the structure of the system; namely, language. The meaning of a sign is simultaneous with its differentiation from other signs. Such a differentiation is operative both on the phonological level (with respect to the signifier) and the semantic level (with respect to the signified). The total sign results from the conjunction of a set of defferentially defined units at the level of the signifier with a set of defferentially defined units at the level of the signified. So the sign is the result of a double articulation.

Once the meaning of a sign is shown not to be dependent on a bi-polar relation but constituted by a fabric of differences, it becomes increasingly more difficult to conceive of a system of images and objects whose signifieds can exist independently of language. To perceive what a sign signifies is inevitably to fall back on the individuation of a language; there is no meaning which is not designated, and the world of signifieds is none other than that of language. Meaning is not produced by a dyadic relation between the sign and an ontologically distinct referent. The signified is always *internal* to language. Thus, in this approach to semiology, language is the perspective of perception, which, as Roland Barthes has put it, "yields meanings" (*S/Z* 3-16). Barthes' approach is to include all that is perceptible into one or another system of signs for which meaning is a concomitant function. In this context, the agency of any semiology becomes closely bound to language.

What then of the ontological status of language? Saussure has said that language is not subject to either the individual or social will, although a community of speakers is necessary for the realization of language. It is neither a transcendent reality with respect to all the speaking subjects, nor is it a phantasm formed by the individual. Rather, it can be construed as the point of intersection of speaking and meaning which enables thought to be articulated. Thus, language is not a thing but a system of rules which subsist between the speaking subjects but is never fully realized in any of them. Language is both the product of human beings yet, at the same time, transcends them. For Heidegger, as we have seen, "language speaks not man"; for Saussure language is not subject to the individual speaker. In both thinkers language takes on an almost independent status. Although, on the one hand the structures of language are nothing other than the scientific description of speech acts, and therefore are ontologically dependent on a community of speakers; on the other hand, this community of speakers must in some sense follow the rules of *la langue* even while their patterns are being described. The necessity arises due to the fact that there is no *a priori* or natural rules of language *per se*. The relations between signifiers and signifieds is arbitrary *vis à vis* other languages and thus communication relies upon our following the rules as if they were necessary. Here we have a dialectical situation. Neither is prior to the other, neither can subsist without the other, and neither is independent of the other. Each is necessary for the constitution of meaning and the articulation of thought. At no time can the appropriation of language by the speaking subject allow language itself to become an object, even for the linguist, who must speak in order to carry on his enterprise. Subjects don't use language(s) as if they were outside of language because, as centers of consciousness, subjects are always already constituted linguistically. The words that I speak are encompassed within a sphere of meaning. Each speaking subject through the articulation of signs is integrated into the collectivity of speaking subjects. As this integration takes place, the speaking subject inscribes him/herself in the system of differences which constitutes a language.

Derrida has acknowledged that Saussure provided us with the insight that taken singly, signs do not signify anything, that each of them does not so much express a meaning as a "mark," a divergence of meaning between itself and other signs. As we have seen, the system of signs is constituted by the differences between terms and not by their fullness; meaning is not transparent, contained and present within the individual signifier. The process of signification is dependent upon a network of oppositions and not a consolidated central core. However, Derrida is also critical of what he sees as inherently metaphysical elements in Saussure's structuralism which I would now like to explore, in order to effect the transition from structuralism to deconstruction.

> The science of linguistics determines language: its field of objectivity: in the last instance and in the irreducible simplicity of its essence, as the unity of the *phone*, the *glossa*, and the *logos*. This determination is by rights anterior to all the eventual differentiations that could arise within the systems of terminology of the different schools (language / speech) [langue / parole]; code / message; scheme / usage; linguistic / logic . . . the immediate and privileged unity which founds significance and acts of language is the articulated unity of sound and sense within the phonie. With regard to this unity, writing would always to derivative, accidental, particular, exterior, doubling the signifier: phonetic. (*Grammatology* 29)

In keeping with Plato and Aristotle, Saussure also maintains a merely derivative place for writing: "Language and writing are two distinct systems of signs; the second exists for the sole purpose of representing the first" (*General Linguistics* 23). Also, "The linguistic object is not defined by the combination of the written word and the spoken word: the spoken form alone constitutes the object" (45). Given that Saussure has already constituted the sign in terms of the relation between sound-image and concept, writing can do no other than be relegated to a subordinate role, a mere representation of the spoken word. Of course, this relation of writing and speech, where the former already constitutes an outside or exterior position, is to reaffirm the binary oppositions which lie at the heart of the metaphysical tradition. To bequeath an equal status to writing would be to enact a type of violence *vis à vis* the tradition; it would be to disturb and threaten the security of the natural relation. As Derrida remarks:

> This tone began to make itself heard when, at the moment of already tying the *episteme* and the *logos* within the same possibility, the *Phaedrus* denounced writing as the intrusion of an artful technique, a forced entry of a totally original sort, an archetypal violence: eruption of the *outside* within the *inside*, breaking into the interiority of the soul, the living self-presence of the soul within the true logos. (*Grammatology* 34)

Derrida intends to deconstruct this tradition by showing why "the violence of writing does not *befall* an innocent language" (3-7) because language already has the structure of writing. It is important to note the broader ramifications of this deconstruction. Derrida connects "phonocentrism" to logocentrism and thus the displacement of the spoken word in favor of writing is also a displacement of the self-presence of rational consciousness. As Spivak points out, we must be careful not to construe writing in its narrow sense as "graphic notation on tangible material" (lxix). What becomes pertinent is a recognition of the features of "writing-in-general": "the absence of the author, and of the subject matter, interpretability and the deployment of space and time" (lxix). We already recognize these features in writing in the narrow sense, yet we ignore the fact that everything else manifests the same characteristics.

Saussure is clear that the linguistic sign is "a two-sided psychological entity" (66) and it is precisely this belief which, to determine the "exact place of semiology" (66) one must consult the psychologist, that Derrida finds problematic. Writing, inasmuch as it displaces the control of the subject—the signatory who is absent—allows for the transmutation of language without consulting the will of the productive consciousness. Derrida argues that:

> The thesis of the arbitrariness of the sign . . . indirectly but irrevocably contests de Saussure's declared proposition when he chases writing to the outer darkness of language. This thesis successfully accounts for a conventional relationship between the phoneme and the grapheme . . . but by the same token it forbids that the latter be an 'image' of the former. (*Grammatology* 45)

There is no "natural" relation holding between phoneme and grapheme that would warrant privileging the first term and relegating the latter to the dependent role of "image" or "representation."

> In fact, even within so-called phonetic writing, the 'graphic' signifier refers to the phoneme through a web of many dimensions which binds it, like all signifiers, to other written and oral signifiers, within a 'total' system open, let us say, to all possible investments of sense. We must begin with the possibility of that total system. (45)

Derrida expands the discussion of Saussure's notions of difference and the arbitrariness of the sign through the deployment of what he terms the "instituted trace" (46). There is never a sign which carries meaning within itself; rather, there is a continual deferral to other signs. Meaning is produced precisely at this point of difference: "the trace, where the relationship with the other is marked, articulates its possibility in the entire field of the entity" (47). Thus, the sign, as Spivak puts it, is always "inhabited" by other signs which do not present themselves as such; there is always a deferral to something absent. This absence of the transcendental signified is what Derrida refers to as "play," couched in terms of a deconstruction of traditional ontology which would insist upon a determinant exterior referent for each individualized and fully present signifier.

Derrida argues that "by definition, difference is never in itself a sensible plenitude" (*Grammatology* 53). Thus, it cannot be the case that there is a "naturally phonic essence of language" (53). But if this is the case, Saussure's relegation of writing to the periphery, dependent upon speech, is unwarranted.

> On the one hand, the phonic element, the term, the plenitude that is called sensible, would not appear as such without the difference or opposition which gives them *form*. Such is the most evident significance of the appeal to difference as the reduction of phonic substance. Here the appearing and functioning of difference presupposes an originary synthesis not preceded by any absolute simplicity. Such would be the originary trace. Without a retention in the minimal unit of temporal experience. Without a trace retaining the other as other in the same, no difference would do its work and no meaning would appear. It is not the question of a constituted difference here, but rather, before all determination of the content, of the *pure* movement which produces difference. *The (pure) trace is differance.* (62)

Différance becomes the condition for fullness and plenitude. Due to its trace-structure, writing or "arch-writing," as Derrida calls it, exposes or makes manifest the operation of *différance*, the play of differences. *Différance* has the function both of delaying and differing. The silent nature of the "a" "refers us to an order that resists philosophy's founding opposition between sensible and intelligible" (*Speech and Phenomena*). *Différance*, marks a deferment in time and a differentiation of distinction in space.

Before turning to the operation of *différance* in more detail, I would like to consider Susan Handelman's discussion of the relation between *écriture*, as Derrida defines it, and some of the more radical presuppositions of rabbinic teaching. Certain notions which appear in the rabbinic tradition—interpretation, otherness, and displacement—have already been evoked above. Others, such as exile and namelessness, will be further discussed, in relation to Levinas ("Deconstruction and Praxis"). Thus, despite a *prima facie* response on the part of the reader that this insertion may be somewhat gratuitous, I believe that it is useful to the development of our overall project.

At the beginning of "Ellipsis," Derrida writes:

> Here or there we have discerned writing: a nonsymmetrical division designated on the one hand the closure of the book, and on the other the opening of the text. On the one hand the theological encyclopedia and, modeled upon it, the book of man. On the other a fabric of traces marking the disappearance of an exceeded God or of an erased man. The question of writing could be opened only if the book was closed. The joyous wandering of the grapheïn then became wandering without return. The opening into the text was adventure without reserve. (*Writing and Difference* 294)

According to Handelman, writing, construed by Derrida as the free-play of the grapheïn, which defies phonocentric attempts to arrest its metonymic charge, is prefigured in rabbinic thought. Similar to Heidegger's "new" experience with language, the rabbinic interpretive posture displaces the search for identity and presence, indicative of the onto-theological tradition (identified in what follows as concomitant with the Graeco-Christian tradition): "For the Rabbis, Writing, the Text, not only precedes speech but precedes the entire natural world. Rabbinic thought does not move from the sensible to the ideal transcendent signified but from the sensible to the Text" (104). In contrast to the Platonic desire to realize the non-linguistic referent of the signifier in a transcendent signified, "for the Rabbis, interpretation, not incarnation, is the central divine act" (104). Handelman further points out, that unlike Greek logic, the subject / predicate relation (which has proved a formidable barrier against the possibility of thinking being in non-entitative terms), in Hebrew, is not connected by the copular.

> Hebrew does not have any form of the verb 'to be' in the present tense. Predicative utterances are linguistically constructed through the juxtaposition of nominal forms in a free-order—and this linguistic structure may underlie the Rabbinic logical principle of predication by juxtaposition. (104)

This displacement of presence, coupled with the associative and metonymic structure of the Hebrew language, effectively privileges the absent. Furthermore, as Handelman notes, hearing rather than seeing becomes the dominant mode of disclosure, and thus, automatically undermines the tradition's concern with resemblance and representation in the search for identity (105). The reification of the word is absent from rabbinic thought. As Handelman writes, "Meaning is not sought in a non-linguistic realm external to the text. Language and the text, to use Derridean terminology, are the place and play of differences, and truth as conceived by the Rabbis was not an instantaneous unveiling of the One, but a continuing process of interpretation" (106). What becomes important for our purposes in the experience of the Jew is this radical loss of place, an existence without identity. Existing always on the margins, at the boundary between presence and absence, the more extreme varieties of rabbinic teaching can be seen as a paradigmatic model of non-logocentric intervention. As Handelman puts it: "The Jew is unreconciled: he exists in the realm of desire, difference, and displacement—not fulfillment, identification and unity" (109).

Now, while it is not my intention to debate to what extent Handelman is correct in superimposing Derrida on the rabbinic tradition, her parallels do seem striking. What concerns me more, is that if the points of coalescence are persuasive, we may have yet one more point of intervention in our attempt to disrupt our logocentric world. If Derrida believes that "the thought of Levinas can make us tremble" (cited in Handelman, 114), then perhaps we cannot easily ignore it.

> Parmenides' disregard of the Other is 'totalitarian' and tautologous, according to Levinas and Derrida, and the rebellion against the Greeks is a species of liberation. (114)

We have already seen that Derrida insists that inverting the hierarchical ranking of phoneme over grapheme has an inherent liberating effect—both textually and, I would argue, politically. There seems to me to be no great disparity between textual violence and political violence. Both forms deploy the same desire for autonomy, identity, and sovereignty. Handelman writes that "like Writing, the Jew is historically the castigated other, intruder, threat, scapegoat, exile, idolater . . ." (117). If the Jew resists the tradition's desire to "pin / pen down" the trace, opting rather to dwell in the space opened by the play of difference, then our deconstructive strategies can only benefit from an encounter with rabbinic thought. Of course, we must be careful not to nonchalantly impute Derrida's desire to *remain* in exile to all forms of rabbinic thought. Handelman points out that Derrida's is a "specific form of Jewish heresy" (122). There is no hope of a return to or of an "origin"; there is no "lure of the origin, the end, the line, the ring, the volume, the center" (*Writing and Difference* 295). Exile and non-identity are affirmed, not mourned. This notion of exile, will be reassessed in the final chapter in light of our particular concern: nationalism. In a sense, it will be deployed as both a response and a refusal; a response to otherness and a refusal to categorize or identify the self. For now, I will return to consider in more detail how the play of differences operates in the production of a text.

2. French Anti-Humanism: Decentering the Subject

In her introduction to Derrida's *Dissemination*, Barbara Johnson writes:

> if the traditional logic of meaning as an unequivocal structure of mastery is Western metaphysics, the deconstruction of metaphysics cannot simply combat logocentric meaning by opposing some other meaning to it. *Différance* is not a concept or "idea" that is truer than presence. It can only be a process of textual work, a strategy of *writing*.
> (xvi)

Derrida's notion of *différance* (despite the difficulties of which he is acutely aware) cannot be reduced to a governing metaphysical principle. He writes, "Not only is '*différance*' irreducible to every ontological or theological-onto-theological reappropriation, but it opens up the very space in which onto-theology: philosophy: produces its systems and its history. It thus encompasses and irrevocably surpasses onto-theology or philosophy. (*Speech and Phenomena* 135).

At its heart lie time and history:

> In marking out *différance*, everything is a matter of strategy and risk. It is a question of strategy because no transcendent truth present outside the sphere of writing can theoretically command the totality of this field. It is hazardous because this strategy orients the tactics according to a final aim, a telos or the theme of domination, a mastery or an ultimate reappropriation of movement and

field. In the end, it is a strategy without finality. (*Speech and Phenomena* 135)

Différance gestures toward the temporalizing activity of language. *Différance* is not to be construed simply as a concept but as the "possibility of conceptuality, of the conceptual system and process in general" (140). *Différance* is, as Derrida observes, the condition for the possibility of *any* discourse and "can no longer be understood according to the concept of 'sign,' which has always been taken to mean the representation of a presence and has been constituted in a system (of thought or language) determined on the basis of and in view of presence" (138).

    Différance always leads back to the ontological difference. Being is never simply presence, but the movement from absence to presence. "Its" figures are always finite, constrained by a discourse and determined by a context which are both historically and culturally situated. The hierarchical ranking of discourses and the kind of ascension that typifies the Western metaphysical tradition (since Plato) is being resisted. Discourse is transitory, finite, and historically situated thus, *a fortiori*, truth, including the truth of the self, suffers the same fate. Yet, the "will to truth," the desire to capture and grasp a univocal meaning, whether technological or onto-theological, continues to hold us in its grip. But truth, knowledge, objectivity and all other attendant notions are inherently tied to interpretation. No discourse, not even that concerning the constitution of subjectivity is innocent of "ulterior motives." All discourse is inextricably tied to the political conditions of a culture at any point in its history.

    In *S/Z*, Barthes has argued that the "I" which approaches the text is already a plurality of other texts, "of codes which are infinite or more precisely, lost (whose origin is lost)" (10). It has been the tendency of metaphysics, as was demonstrated above, to construe the "I " as fully present, complete—an identical point of origin for the disclosure of the world. By "pluralizing" the "I," Barthes show that subjectivity is not an "innocent" entity, somehow anterior to the text, but always already constitutes a point of view, a perspective which is deeply embedded within culture and thoroughly contextual. Barthes writes,

> 'Objectivity' and 'subjectivity' are of course forces which
> can take over a text, but they are forces which have no
> affinity with it. Subjectivity is a plenary image, with which
> I may be thought to encumber the text, but whose
> deceptive plenitude is merely the wake of all codes which
> constitute me, so that my subjectivity has ultimately the
> generality of stereotypes. (10)

Understanding a text is always a *productive* act. The
recuperation of meaning of the text, however, never takes place
within a plane of neutrality. A dominant voice always takes over,
insists on being heard. In a certain sense we are incapable of
escaping such domination. The hegemony of logocentrism which
pervades Western discourse, cornering the market, appears well
entrenched and implacable. Yet, the site is becoming less secure.
The deployment of deconstructive strategies threatens to displace,
dislodge, threatens to intervene—exploding metaphysical
security, releasing texts form their traditional bondage to the
desire for a univocal reading. Derrida's disseminational approach
disrupts the specious present. Manifest meanings (signifieds) are
always on the brink of being exploded. The latent meanings,
provisionally repressed, stand ready to be disclosed, dissipating
the smoke-screen.

> Dissemination endlessly opens up a 'snag' in writing that
> can no longer be mended, a spot where neither meaning,
> however plural, nor any form of presence can pin / pen
> down (*agrapher*) the trace. Dissemination treats: doctors:
> that 'point' the movement of significance would regularly
> come to "tie down" the play of the trace, thus producing (a)
> history. The security of each point arrested in the name of
> the law is hence blown up. (Dissemination 26)

Derrida's insistence on the radical overdetermination of
every signifier opens the space for an intervention into the text,

explodes the security of the interior, allows the repressed to become manifest. To delay / defer recuperation is, however, immensely difficult. How then to proceed? What might our strategy be? To disrupt the hegemony of a dominant code makes one vulnerable to the risk of substituting another code, equally as restrictive, equally metaphysical. The subversion can never be completed or finalized, it must be incessant and without arche. Derrida writes, "If there is thus no thematic unity or overall meaning to re-appropriate beyond the textual instances, no total message located in some imaginary order, intentionality or lived experience, the text is no longer the expression or representation (felicitous or otherwise) of any 'truth' that would come to diffract or assemble itself in the polysemy of literature. It is this hermeneutic concept of polysemy that must be replaced by dissemination (213-214).

Rodolphe Gasche has argued, (and the parallel is an interesting one) that the "Derridean word 'text' is, in fact, 'a translation (without translation) of the Heideggerian word 'being'" (160). In both cases the inquiry into text or being should not be conceived as an inquiry into something that could be encountered in an empirical experience, nor with some idealized totality (as the sum total of all things or the sum total of all inscriptions). "The transcendental experience of the text is, indeed," Derrida points out, "neither the experience of a universal and eidetic *object* nor simply a repetition of a *transcendental experience* in either a Kantian or Husserlian sense" (*Dissemination* 213-214). How then are we to speak of Derrida's notion of text and textuality?

When we speak of the world as text or when we speak of a textualizing of the world, we are not performing an ontological reduction of phenomena to the primacy of the word. We are merely insisting that world never is disclosed as a whole, transparent and fully present. We are never concerned with what might be construed as the "common sense" notion of an external reality. The world never presents itself in terms of a pre-articulated, self-differentiating system of objects. The world and its history are inaccessible to us except in textual form; any experience that we can communicate or speak about necessarily presupposes language, modes of conceptual disclosure and discursive frameworks. As Derrida has said, logocentrism can be identified as the "exigent, powerful, systematic, and irrepressible desire" for a "transcendental signified," a decontextualized "given" (*Grammatology* 49). We have already seen Heidegger's response to such a naive realism.

In a sense, it is the placing of speech and communication as the essence of language that blinds us to the fact that the "transcendental signified" is an illusion. The "thing itself always escapes." The sign is inherently a trace. If there is a referral, it is to something absent; another sign that does not appear as such. Thus, we can generate an infinite regression to a previous moment of signification. There is no origin of meaning, no absolute presence of meaning, and no ultimate and unitary meaning: "The sign cannot be taken as a homogeneous unit bridging an origin (referent) and an end (meaning)" (49).

Unlike structuralism which is based upon the notion of a centered structure which permits only a limited number of combinations and therefore gives closure to the text, Derrida calls attention to the notion of *structuralité de la structure* (structured structure). Because the center is continually displaced during deconstructive analysis, the analysis also constitutes a critique of the center itself. It is in a similar fashion that Heidegger gestures toward a certain absence, a withdrawing of being. The event that he terms *Ereignis* is precisely this crossing out of being; being is put under erasure. "Being" does not signify a transcendental referent; it marks a movement, a deferral; it must be understood *sous rature* (under erasure). Only by an act of violence can one force being to yield a referent.

We have already said that Derrida's strategies rely upon an undermining of the notion of hierarchy. This is nowhere more evident than his analysis in *Dissemination* of Mallarmé's *Mimique* to which I would like to turn in order to give an illustration of those strategies in operation. Gasche notes that *Mimique*, "deconstructs the Platonic values of truth and reference of mimesis as subject to those values" (166).

Derrida draws an interesting parallel with Goedel when he states that

> An undecideable proposition, as Goedel demonstrated in 1931, is a proposition which, given a system of axioms governing a multiplicity, is neither an analytical nor deductive consequence of those axioms, nor in contradiction with them, neither true nor false with respect to those axioms. *Tertium datur*, without synthesis. (*Dissemination* 219)

The key word is of course "undecideability." There appears no way of "pinning down" precisely what is being represented in Mallarmé's text. This effect or "after-effect" produced by the text is a result, in part at least, of overturning the traditional priority of the semantic over the syntactic, in much the same way as Foucault's genealogies trace at the micrological level the various practices that inscribe the human body, rather than concentrating on an identity which metaphysics sees as essential to selfhood. Thus, Derrida and Foucault privilege the syntactic over the semantic and the micrological over the macrological respectively. They both resist the tendency to construct over-arching structures which attempt to subsume the complexity of their respective data under a particular master-code or master-narrative. Derrida writes,

> it is not the lexical richness, the semantic infiniteness of a word or concept, its depth or breadth, the sedimentation that has produced inside it two contradictory layers of signification (continuity and discontinuity, inside and outside, identity and difference, etc.). What counts here is the formal or syntactical *praxis* that composes and decomposes it. (*Dissemination* 212)

The event narrated by the mime of *Mimique* is a "hymen" (a point of suspension, an "in-between"), the marriage of Pierrot and Colombine. This marriage culminates in Pierrot's subsequent assassination of his wife by tickling her to death (that is to say, by means of a perfect crime which leaves no traces) and on Pierrot's own death in front of the laughing portrait of his victim (a death which will not show any traces, either). The two deaths, resulting from an orgastic spasm, represents Pierrot's and Columbines consummation of their marriage. As Gasche points out, the "miming of this event in which nothing has taken place exhibits the textual structure of Mallarmé's *Mimique*" (165). As Derrida writes, "It is a dramatization which illustrates nothing, which illustrates the *nothing*, lights up a space, re-marks a spacing as nothing, a blank: while as a yet unwritten page, blank as the difference between two lines" (*Dissemination* 236-237). It is a mime that refers only to itself; a presentation of theatrical space. Signs that refer only to other signs; but there is more: "A writing that refers back only to itself carries us at the same time, indefinitely and systematically, to some other writing" (202). The process is infinite, despite the fact that we choose to stop somewhere. For Derrida then, what Mallarmé has "captured" is the fact that metaphysical interpretation which would stop at the *thing* imitated is an illusion. Again to quote Gasche: "Signs in the text of *Mimique* are made to refer to what according to metaphysics is only derived, unreal, unpresent. . ." (165). This doubling of the sign is what Derrida calls "re-marking." In contrast to a traditional philosophy of language that would attribute some signified, full and present, to each textual instance, Derrida poses the "logic of the hymen." For the reader of a deconstructed text such as Mallarmé's *Mimique*, this effects a sort of suspension, a temporary loss of place, and this is Derrida's "intention": "the hymen, the confusion between the present and the nonpresent along with all the indifferences it entails within the whole series of opposites . . . what counts here is the *between*, the in-between-ness of the hymen" (240). Like *différance*, the operation of the hymen, the "between" becomes the possibility of conceptuality, both syntactically and semantically.

> Through the re-marking of its semantic void, it in fact begins to signify: its semantic void signifies spacing and articulation; it has as its meaning the possibility of syntax;

it orders the play of meaning. Neither purely syntactic nor purely semantic, it marks the articulated opening of that opposition. (202)

As such, the parallel to Heidegger's *Ereignis* can provisionally be drawn. To speak of the hymen / *différance* becomes equally as difficult as speaking of *Ereignis*. Both defy conceptualization. Neither can be ordered in terms of metaphysically constituted grammatical structures. In both cases it, is the historicity of being that is being thought. However, as Gasche asserts, there are differences between the thinkers which may be more significant than a change of style (realizing of course that tone and style are essential to the conceptual process and not extrinsic to it). Given that Heidegger's thinking is almost exclusively concerned with the question of being, it remains firmly entrenched within the context of questions traditionally voiced by metaphysics, despite the fact that the inquiry into the ontological difference is an approach to the meaning of being which defies all metaphysical determinations.

As Caputo has argued in a yet unpublished paper, "From the Deconstruction of Hermeneutics to the Hermeneutics of Deconstruction," Derrida is sharply critical of hermeneutics as a philosophy of meaning. Meanings are constituted by their place in the system of differences, but that place is held precariously and is subject to an infinite number of "shadings off" or blurring of boundaries. Derrida wants to subvert the primacy of meaning by systematically exploring all the surfaces of language, all the possible graphic, phonic, etymological, rhythmic and psychoanalytic linkages among words. But Derrida does not, it must be remembered, undermine the semantic to *replace* it with various types of syntactic differentiation. The move he makes is a displacement rather than a surpassing; it is an acknowledgment that things could have been otherwise. Thus, while Heidegger initiates the critical posture to the metaphysics of presence, it is Derrida who pushes it to a far more extreme strategy. For Derrida, Heidegger's discussion of "authenticity" and the "meaning of being" is rife with metaphysical complicities, with nostalgia.

"There will be no unique name, not even the name of Being. It must be conceived without "nostalgia," that is, it must be conceived outside the myth of the purely maternal or paternal language belonging to the lost fatherland of thought" (*Speech and Phenomena* 159). Derrida does not desire to retrieve what was lost in metaphysics but make it "tremble" (*ébranler*), which is what he means by "solicitation." Such strategies require the overturning of the supremacy of the semantic over the syntactic as the first phase. Language becomes essentially "tropic." Tropes cease to be understood aesthetically, as Paul de Man has noted in *Allegories of Reading*, and they are not to be conceived either semantically, as figurative meanings that derive from literal, proper denominations, or as mere ornaments. De Man argues that "the trope is not a derived, marginal, or aberrant form of language but the linguistic paradigm *par excellence*. The figurative structure is not one linguistic mode among many but characterizes language as such" (Allegories 105).

We have seen then, that from the Sausserian emphasis on the role of differential structures operative within language, Derrida has been able to effect a radical overturning of the metaphysical hierarchizing of such binary oppositions as speech / writing, sensible / intelligible, and so forth. The deployment of terms such as trace, *différance*, dissemination and hymen, reveal termporalization as indicative of all modes of disclosure of our world. The displacement of meaning constitutes a twofold rupture *vis à vis* the tradition. First, any attempt to impose a master-narrative upon the reading of a text or the reading of the history of a culture, cannot be enacted without a violent imposition, a closure of the possibility of interpretation—the rationale for which entails certain ideological complicities. Second, and this will be our concern in the next chapter, "The Self and Power," when closure does take place it is always a product of particular historical configurations of power. While Derrida is concerned with exposing such impositions—as was Heidegger—through a destruction / deconstruction of the Euro-western philosophical tradition, Foucault concentrates his attention on a genealogical survey of post-Enlightenment thought in both the philosophical and non-philosophical domains. Derrida has argued that

> If words and concepts receive meaning only in sequences of differences, one can justify one's language, and one's choice of terms only within a topic (an orientation in space) and a historical strategy. The justification can therefore never be absolute and definitive. It corresponds to a condition of forces and translates an historical calculation. (*Grammatology* 70)

It is an analysis of the particular historical configurations that constitute the modern epoch that we now turn.

The Self and Power

1. Normalization and the Strategies of Social Control

> By the introduction of labor the depth of desire entered in place of intimacy; and from the very start, there entered in place of its release from bondage a form of rational enchainment in which the truth of the moment is no longer of import, but only the end result of any set of operations: in short, the first labor establishes the world of objects . . . since the foundation of the world of objects, the human being himself becomes one among the objects of this world, at least for the period during which one labors. (Bataille 88)

While Foucault (unlike Bataille) is not concerned with the "origin" of the objectified self, he is concerned to examine, in microscopic detail, the modes of objectification that have infused the human subject and continue to constitute the self. Such modes are inherently tied to relations of power and control. As Nietzsche saw the "will to power" and the "will to truth" as two sides of the same coin; for Foucault, there is an inextricable reciprocity between power and knowledge.

Despite the fact that, for Foucault, power cannot be construed merely in terms of the coercive forces of a dominant class (as one finds in Marxism), he is undeniably aware (as I suggested in the Introduction) that the task of embarking upon an economy of power relations will have the effect of identifying and dispersing, in the socio-political arena, areas in which power relations have become coagulated to an extent which forms centers of domination and subjection. Thus, while, power relations are an internal phenomenon, constitutive of the social fabric, their effects can be either positive or negative. A precise determination and genealogical analysis of the negative aspects of power that manifest themselves in terms of policies of exclusion and marginalization can be resisted both in the sense of an exposé (as we discussed in Chapter One) as well as a more confrontational posture. These postures are not mutually exclusive. Whether the intervention is discursive or non-discursive will depend upon the context and the particular nature of the power relations in question. What I must insist upon is that Foucault believes that "we can recognize that certain power relations function in such a way as to constitute, globally, an effect of domination" (Politics and Ethics 378). Genealogical analyses can allow us to better understand *how* these effects are produced.

In this chapter, the relation between language (discursive formations), self, and structure will again be addressed. In the second part of the chapter I will argue that Foucault's genealogical method can provide the social and cultural critic with an invaluable tool.

It could be argued that the *Archaeology of Knowledge* can be seen as an elucidation and "working out" of the themes presented in *The Order of Things*. Foucault addresses, in a more systematic fashion, concepts such as discontinuity, rupture, threshold, limit, series, and transformation in the history of ideas, which were introduced in the earlier work. At the outset, we must be clear that although Foucault sees history as marked by discontinuous moments, (which cannot be subsumed under any over-arching *telos*), he believes that change in history is the radical transformation of the relations among the parts of society and not *creatio ex nihilo*. Among the most important concepts which Foucault critiques are those of "tradition" and the notion that there exists an underlying continuity in the light of which it becomes possible to isolate the "new," to "transfer its merits to originality, to genius, to the decisions proper to individuals"

(*Archaeology* 21). Foucault is uneasy with respect to the primacy given to "subjectivity," an unease which will develop into an attempt to displace the subject in the history of ideas. Foucault will use his typical methodological rigor or "relentless erudition" to subject terms such as "unity," "identity," "spirit," etc., to a radical critique. Similarly, the traditional and supposedly manifest distinctions between science, literature, philosophy, religion, history, and fiction will be analyzed and not presupposed. Here, Foucault is at one with Derrida in the refusal to embrace the traditional ranking of these categories. Foucault believes that these distinctions are "normative rules," "institutional types," and have no universally recognizable characteristics. Thus, the way these disciplines articulated the field of discourse in the 17th and 18th centuries is significantly different from the way they articulate discourse today. Unfortunately, we still articulate our political discourse in terms of categories drawn from an earlier era which are outmoded and obsolete. I am arguing that we must rethink what constitutes the social bond and political existence.

The book and the "*oeuvre*" offer paradigmatic examples that illustrate our concern with "unities" which are thought to be autonomous, self-contained wholes. It would appear that given the material individuation of the book, we can be secure in the belief that it constitutes a distinct entity with clearly defined parameters. But, Foucault argues,

> The frontiers of a book are never clear-cut; beyond the title, the first lines, and the last full stop, beyond its internal configurations and its autonomous form, it is caught up in a system of references to other books, other texts, other sentences: it is a node within a network. (23)

Foucault echoes Derrida's insistence that a text always contains a trace of something that has already occurred, a referral to other texts which are absent. This intertextuality is broadened by Foucault to include the social, economic and political spheres. In a similar fashion what one is to include within a particular "oeuvre" is equally problematized. To give an example, the relation of the name "Nietzsche" to the early scholastic dissertations is not the same relation as that which exists between the name and "Zarathustra." Now, Foucault is not denying that a unity exists; he is denying that such a unity is self-evident. Thus, to speak of a Nietzschean mement within the history of ideas, and to suggest that the term "Nitzschean" designates a particular body of thought, is to forget or fail to recognize that what we decide to subsume under the term is the result of an interpretive operation and is not manifestly evident: therefore, ". . . the *oeuvre* can be regarded neither as an immediate unity, nor as a homogeneous unity" (24). We can already see what possible consequences would ensue if we substitute "subjectivity" or "self" for "*oeuvre*" or "book." Just as the latter terms are not the result of discerning a self-evident presence, an autonomous "unity," neither is the self. Rather than uncritically accepting the notion of "unity" and then presupposing that we can explain other terms in the light of it, we should subject this notion itself to close scrutiny. We must raise questions such as: What is it? How can it be defined? What articulation is it capable of? The task then, Foucault argues, will be to accept the groupings that history suggests only for the purposes of interrogation, analysis, and for discovering the conditions which allow for their emergence. One is led, therefore, "to the project of a pure description of discursive events as the horizon for the search for the unities that form within it" (27). However, Foucault is clear that this description is to be distinguished from an analysis of language in the traditional sense:

> The question posed by language analysis of some discursive fact or other is always: according to what rules has a particular statement been made, and consequently according to what rules could similar statements be made? The description of the events of discourse poses a quite different question: how is it that one particular statement appeared rather than another? (27)

Foucault desires to undermine the traditional interest in intention and hidden meanings: "we must grasp the statement in the exact specificity of its occurrence" (28), determine the conditions of its existence and to what extent and in what way it excludes other statements. Foucault's project is the inherently empirical one of explicating the cultural conditions that allow the emergence of a particular discourse. Unlike the usual elements of linguistics (semantics, syntax, pragmatics, etc.) discourse is, for Foucault, susceptible to analysis in relation to other aspects of social life, politics, culture, economic, and social institutions.

What becomes of interest for our purposes is the way in which this elucidation of the "enunciative field" (a referential network of statements) relates to structures of power. The enunciative field involves certain forms of co-existence which "outline a field of presence," a sort of referential matrix involving statements judged to be true within that matrix and also those that are criticized or rejected. In studying the economy of discursive constellations, their regulation and function, one is in a position to view, as it were, the emergence of particular conceptual configurations which elucidate the field that allowed them to exist as dominant discourses, imbued with the capacity to produce truth (including the truth of the subject) and further to bring into play knowledges that were subjected or rejected.

For Foucault, each society has its own "regime" of truth, that is, the type of discourse which it accepts and makes function as true. In our society it could be argued that science and scientific discourse have been awarded that role, as Heidegger has suggested. Power is exercised via an integrated process of normalization where "normalization" denotes the acquisition by the subject of a particular discourse.

In our own case, the social body becomes *technologically* encoded. The body is subjected to a host of regulatory disciplines: medical, legal, physical, and psychological. One of the most important results of Foucault's research is to demonstrate that, fundamentally, power (the action of one body upon another) should not be construed as the privilege of a particular class (although of course at any time a particular class may be in a position to manipulate power structures), but that the "micro-mechanisms" of power determine relations at every level. Foucault is clear that these mechanisms function primarily not by virtue of legislation but far more pervasively through a technology of normalization. We find the following in *The History of Sexuality*:

> The society that emerged in the 19th century . . . did not confront sex with a fundamental refusal of recognition. On the contrary, it put into operation an entire machinery for producing true discourses concerning it. Not only did it speak of sex and compel everyone to do so; it also set out to formulate the uniform truth of sex. As if it was essential that sex be inscribed not only in an economy of pleasure but in an ordered system of knowledge. Thus sex gradually became an object of great suspicion; the general and disquieting meaning that pervades our conduct and our existence, in spite of ourselves. (69)

We err if we believe that we have been liberated from the tyrannical sexual oppression indicative of the 19th century. Foucault believes that such liberation is an illusion. Due to the rapid (at least since Freud) production of discourses concerning sexuality, especially within the domain of medicine and psycho-analysis, the desire to unmask its true essence has become one of the focal points of our lives. Thus, "We must not think that by saying yes to sex, one says no to power; on the contrary, one tracks along the course laid out by the general deployment of sexuality" (157). The sexual encoding of our bodies via the truth of "sex" and the knowledge of "sex," is a product of certain economy of power, of normalization. The pluralizing of discourses concerning sexuality create certain types of desire which in turn bring into play, certain types of control. For Foucault the counter-attack against this deployment of sexuality "ought not to be sex-desire but bodies and pleasures" (157). We should cease the "endless task of forcing its secret, of exacting the truest of confessions from a shadow" (159).

Now, the sexual is only one trajectory, only one form of normalization which traverses the body of the subject. In the "Two Lectures," Foucault states that he is mainly concerned with explicating the nature of that power which is capable of producing discourses that are able to exercise such a process of normalization as there "can be no possible exercise of power without a certain economy of discourses of truth which operates through and on the basis of this association" (*Power/Knowledge* 93). But this enterprise can never be conducted universally. Foucault argues in *The Archaeology of Knowledge* that in archaeological analysis comparison is always limited and regional. It attempts to outline particular configurations rather than reveal general forms of power. It is important to note the specificity of Foucault's enterprise, which is incapable of describing an entire world-view. There is no necessity that every discursive formation will exhibit the same field of relations. Such networks cannot be defined in advance of the investigation itself: "the horizon of archaeology is not a science, a rationality, a mentality, a culture; it is rather a tangle of interpositivities whose limits or points of intersection cannot be fixed in a single operation" (93). Thus, Foucault denies the position held by, as he puts it, the friends of the *Weltanschauung*, there is no overarching analysis. The archaeological method is inherently regional in its scope, it is multi-layered and extremely intricate.

Archaeology discerns several possible levels of events operative within discourse. First, there is the level of the appearance of "objects," the types of enunciation, concepts and strategic choices. Second, we have the level of the derivation of new rules that are already in operation. Finally, there is the level at which the substitution of one discursive formation for another takes place. The last level constitutes a variety of what we have referred to as "exclusion"; for our purposes, the exclusion of all that does not conform to the aims and interest of a dominant power structure within a culture.

For Foucault, rather than merely referring to the "living force of change," archaeology "tries to develop this empty, abstract notion, with a view to according it the analyzable status

of transformation" (*Archaeology* 173). Thus, "The contemporan-
eity of several transformations does not mean their exact
chronological coincidence; each transformation may have its own
particular index of temporal "viscosity" (175). It is not so much
that a temporal figure, say the Enlightenment, "imposes its unity
and empty form on all discourses," rather, the Enlightenment is a
name given to an intricate network of "continuities,
discontinuities, modifications within positivities and discursive
formations that appear and disappear" (176). One must study the
economy of the discursive constellation to which a particular
discourse belongs. Thus, Foucault writes:

> This whole group of relations forms a principle of
> determination that permits or excludes, within a given
> discourse, a certain number of statements. These are
> conceptual systematizations, enunciative series, groups
> and organizations of objects that might have been possible
> but which are excluded by a discursive constellation of a
> higher level and in a higher space. (67)

We have already seen the way that the self is but a
perspective rather than a unique and autonomous point for the
disclosure of the world. The self is fully contextualized by "its"
concerns in the world (Heidegger) and thoroughly situated
historically within certain finite conceptual frameworks. We have
spoken often of the fact that the usefulness of Foucault's
genealogies lies in their ability to provide maps of this textualized
self, to spell out specifically the modes of textualization that
infuse the social body. We have further argued that this mapping
of the power relations can aid us in our attempt to diffuse the
coagulations of power that constitute post-Enlightenment rational
discourse.

Foucault is clear, as we have said before, that the
genealogical method is a positive intervention *vis à vis* relations of
power. In fact genealogy is defined in the "Two Lectures," as "the
union of erudite knowledge and local memories which allows us
to establish a historical knowledge of struggles and to make use of

this knowledge tactically today" (83). Its force, as a mode of intervention at the discursive level, bears a striking resemblance to Derrida's deconstructive strategies. Both attempt to release marginalized modes of disclosure from the oppression of solidified and ideologically infused bodies of knowledge. Speaking of genealogy, Foucault writes:

> What it really does is to entertain the claims to attention of local, discontinuous, disqualified, illegitimate knowledges against the claims of a unitary body of theory which filter, hierarchize and order them in the name of some true knowledge and some arbitrary idea of what constitutes a science and its objects. (83)

Both Foucault and Derrida are clear that their respective interventions do not destroy the center and its knowledge (whether from without or within). Genealogy and deconstruction are concerned with the "insurrection of knowledges against the institutions and against effects of the knowledge and power that invest scientific discourse" (87), for Foucault, and the effects of the metaphysics of presence, for Derrida.

Archaeology and genealogy do not represent two unrelated methodological postures: "'archaeology' would be the appropriate methodology of this analysis of local discursivities, 'genealogy' would be the tactics whereby, on the basis of the descriptions of these local discontinuities, the subjected knowledges which were thus released would be brought into play" (85). Despite then, certain suspicions that Foucault's interest in Nietzsche somehow resulted in a disavowal of the earlier structuralist works (*The Order of Things* and *The Archaeology of Knowledge*), it would appear that those early mappings of the discursive constellations were merely the initial part of the whole project.

Thus, I would like to conclude this part of the chapter with a consideration of one of Foucault's most insightful genealogical analyses—of discipline. I will then show how the genealogical method or the mapping of current micrological power relations could be a useful tool of a transgressive praxis.

2. Discipline

The over-arching question posed by Foucault in *Discipline and Punish* is: how did the prison ("a coercive corporal solitary secret model of the power to punish" (*Discipline* 131)), replace the collective signifying model (e.g. torture as a public spectacle) for the teaching of discipline? From being an art of "unbearable sensations," punishment has become an "economy of suspended rights." Foucault argues that the technology of power is the principle both of the humanization of the penal system and of the knowledge of man. He construes the body-politic as a set of "material elements and techniques that serve as weapons, relays, communication routes and supports for power and knowledge relations" that invest human bodies by turning them into objects of knowledge (28).

According to Foucault, the objective of the 19th century movement for the reform of prisons was to set up a new economy of the power to punish, to assure better distribution of control, in a way more subtle, yet also more widely spread in the social body. The core concept that will allow for the automatic functioning of power is discipline. The Enlightenment discovered the body as an object and target of power.

The notion of "man-the-machine" appears, as Foucault argues, on two distinct yet over-lapping levels: the Cartesian "anatomico-metaphysical register" and the "technico-political register." It is constituted by a set of regulations and empirical methods for controlling and correcting operations of the body. The primary institutions from effecting such control were the school, army, and hospital. The distinction between the useful body and the intelligible body is collapsed, the two poles conjoinging through the notion of "docility": "A body is docile that may be subjected, used, transformed and improved" (136). Although, as Foucault is aware, this was not the first instance in which the body had become the object of such "pressing investment," the scale of control and the interest in individual bodies was unprecedented. The process of "working it individually" by subtly and coercively controlling the mechanism itself, its movement, gestures, attitudes, etc., by manipulating its internal organization, brings into play a veritable plethora of codifying strategies. "These methods, which made possible the meticulous control of the operations of the body, which assured the constant subjection of its forces and imposed upon them a relation of docility, utility, might be called 'disciplines'" (137). Foucault argues that it was at this point in history that the "art of the human body" was born. Subsequently, there developed a policy of coercions directed toward the body, a calculated "manipulation of its gestures, its behavior" (137). The production of docility via a political anatomy, a "mechanics of power," had a dual effect. Discipline at one and the same time increases the forces of the body (in terms of utility) but also diminishes its forces in political terms by creating obedience. Thus we see the establishment of the connection between aptitude and increased domination. However, this process should not be viewed as having its origin in a single consolidated central core. It becomes effective through a multiplicity of minor processes which variously intersect and overlap (education, hospitals, military organizations, etc.).

If we were to elicit any particular concern common to all these processes, it might be that of an obsession with detail, a new "micro-physics of power." The meticulous observation of detail plus the awareness that people can be controlled by this information, gives rise to a complex network of methods and data. Foucault argues that discipline requires enclosure: "the specification of a place heterogeneous to all others and closed in upon itself. It is the protected place of disciplinary monotony" (141). Following the monastic model, the machinery put into place to effect the principle of enclosure has, as its main target the notion of partitioning: "each individual has his own place and each place its individual" (143). The model, then, is basically cellular.

However, its function is not only a supervisory one, of breaking dangerous communications, it also includes establishing a "useful space":

> Disciplinary space tends to be divided into as many sections as there are bodies or elements to be distributed. One must eliminate the effects of imprecise distributions, the uncontrolled disappearance of individuals, their diffuse circulation, their unusable and dangerous coagulation; it was a tactic of anti-desertion, anti-vagabondage, anti-concentration. Its aim was to establish presences and absences, to know where and how to locate individuals, to set up useful communications, to interrupt others, to be able at each moment to supervise the conduct of each individual, to assess it, to judge it, to calculate its qualities or merits. It was a procedure, therefore, aimed at knowing, mastering and using. Discipline organizes an analytical space. (143)

The institution that captures these features of control most adequately is Jeremy Bentham's Panopticon: "Inspection functions ceaselessly. The gaze is alert everywhere" (195). Its primary aim is to assure the automatic functioning of power. The inmate is an active participant. The architectural structure is designed in such a way that it is no longer necessary for those who are exercising power to be overtly manifest: "Bentham laid down the principle that power should be visible and unverifiable" (201). The visible aspect is provided by the erection of a central tower from which the prisoner is spied upon. It is unverifiable because although the prisoner is uncertain whether he is being observed at any particular moment, he knows always that it is a possibility. Thus, "The Panopticon is a machine for dissociating the seen / being seen dyad, in the periphic ring, one is totally seen, without ever seeing; in the central tower, one sees everything without ever being seen" (202). Confronted with the possibility of continual surveillance, the prisoner becomes the "principle of his own subjection" (203). There is little need for corporal methods as the prison assumes responsibility for the constraints of power.

However, as Foucault points out, observation was not the only function of the Panopticon. As we have said above, the notion of discipline also incorporates training and behavioral modification. The Panopticon becomes an ideal place for experimentation. It becomes a space in which people can be analyzed and in which the possibilities of behavioral transformations can be determined: "The Panopticon functions as a kind of laboratory of power. Thanks to its mechanisms of observation it gains in efficiency and in the ability to penetrate into men's behavior; knowledge follows the advances of power, discovering new objects of knowledge over all the surfaces on which power is exercised" (204). The principle of the Panopticon, then, is not restricted to the prison; its scope ranges over hospitals, schools, and workshops, In fact it is efficacious anywhere a particular form of behavior is to be imposed. Thus it is not surprising, as Foucault notes, that the structure of our schools, hospitals, places of work, and prisons share the common characteristics of "regular chronologies," "forced labor," and the pervasive feature of surveillance.

We have seen then that power and knowledge share a mutual reciprocity. I would now like to consider in what way Foucault's genealogical surveys can enable us to both become aware of the normalization techniques that constrain and direct our behavior and where necessary, provide us with some critical tools.

3. Strategies of Resistance

In a recent essay entitled: "The Politics of Historical Interpretation: Discipline and De-Sublimation," Hayden White presents the argument that

> Interpretive conflicts reach a limit as specifically interpretive ones when political power or authority is invoked to resolve them. This suggests that interpretation is an activity which in principle, stands over against political activity in much the same way as that contemplation is seen to stand over against action or theory against practice. (20)

However, he rejects this position, arguing instead for an inherent reciprocity between interpretation and power. "'Pure' interpretation, the disinterested inquiry into anything whatsoever, is unthinkable as an ideal without the presupposition of the kind of activity which politics represents" (120). Hayden White recognizes that the modern social sciences have attempted a "de-rhetoricization" of historical thinking from that kind of narrative prose, indicative of romance and the novel. Social science desires to posit a specific conception of historical reality which, unlike the eschatological religious myths of past epochs, will make our past comprehensible to our understanding. Reason imputes a meaning to history, hoping to avoid or negate what it conceives as the undesirable (perhaps psychologically) consequences of allowing it to remain dense or opaque. In what sense then is Reason's demand satisfiable? It seems evident that the way one makes sense of history is important for determining what political posture one chooses to adopt; what politics one will accept as realistic, practicable, and socially responsible. But what if history makes no sense at all? What criteria are being appealed to that will justify our saying that history is "meaningful?" It would seem as Hayden White points out, "it is often overlooked that the conviction that one can make sense of history stands on the same level of epistemic plausibility as the conviction that it makes no sense whatsoever" (135). George Santayana cautions that those who have no understanding of history are condemned to repeat it. If this comment is to be useful it must be seen in terms, not merely of the study of the past, but how one studies it, to what aim or ideological interest is that study subjected? The study of history is never a neutral enterprise. It is important to understand how we arrived at any particular historical viewpoint and in part this entails an understanding of our culture.

There is a marked coalescence between the perspectives of Heidegger and Foucault inasmuch as both thinkers attempt to elicit or make manifest the internal mechanisms of our culture. Both attempt to diagnose how we arrived where we are. The importance of the above question, as Hubert Dreyfus has argued, lies in the fact that an answer, should one be forthcoming, may help us to

> mitigate the effect of our current technological under-
> standing of reality by no longer taking it as self-evident and
> inevitable. When a culture's understanding of being
> becomes unbearable, relativising its convictions is a first
> step toward a cure. ("Beyond Hermeneutics" 76)

Heidegger's critique of technology is an attempt both to understand how technology works, how it became the dominant field of disclosure of the world in which we find ourselves and, perhaps more importantly, what it does to us. We have seen (Part I, Chapter 2) that *Being and Time* represents, in part, an attempt to understand the "intelligibility" of human activity not from the standpoint of an investigation of consciousness but rather, from an examination of what unifies the practices of the subject. *Dasein* is "thrown" into a pre-disclosed world in a state of what

Heidegger terms *Sorge* (care). In *Being and Time*, Heidegger attempts to construct a topology of *Dasein's* existence. The similarity to Foucault's project is noteworthy. Now although it is not Foucault's intention to construct a fundamental ontology (there is no ontic / ontological split) his aim is to demonstrate that individuals function within pre-disclosed structures (Heidegger's being-in-the-world), although for him it is the body that such structures invest and normalize.

In *Power / Knowledge*, Foucault writes:

> Power relations can materially penetrate the body in depth, without depending even on the mediation of the subject's own representations. If power takes hold of the body, this isn't through its having first to be interiorized in people's consciousness. (186)

The genealogical method employed in such works as the *Birth of the Clinic* and *Discipline and Punish* is a study of the significance of the "micropractices" inscribed in our bodies. What becomes important (for my purposes) is that a topology of these micro-practices helps facilitate an effective resistance, the need to resist pervasive practices whose only end or goal is the efficient ordering of society for the benefit of profit and power. Of course such a project can only be effected by a participant who is both involved in the power relations and at the same time able to distance him/herself and conduct the painstaking historical work of diagnosing the history and organization of our current practices; especially, I would argue, those that constitute such notions as sovereignty and autonomy, the most pernicious relics of bourgeois individualism.

Such an analysis is still to be embarked upon. While there is much debate (as we have seen) on the role of the "subject" in post-modernist discourse, sovereignty and autonomy have not been sufficiently critiqued within the context of international relations. We are still entrenched within the paradigm that perceives international relations in terms of a multiplicity of semi-independent autonomous entities; the Treaty of Westphalia is still the dominant way in which we decide to organize the socio-political constitution of our planet.

Genealogical analysis does not reveal a deep hidden truth that is somehow hidden from our everyday awareness. The power relations are evident and manifest to those who are erudite enough to wish to engage in genealogical analysis, as we have seen in our discussion of *Discipline and Punish*. The project becomes one of assembling evidence (the empirical thrust of Foucault's enterprise) which manifests the tendency of our current social practices which, in effect, turn nature and human beings into resources to be efficiently organized and used. Here, Foucault shares Heidegger's belief that in a technological world-view everything stands in reserve for use and exploitation.

In "Afterword: The Subject and Power" Foucault states that his objective has been "to create a history of the different modes by which, in our culture, human beings are made subjects" (208). In answer to the question, why raise the question of power, Foucault answers:

> for us it is not only a theoretical question, but a part of our experience. I'd like to mention only two 'pathological forms': those two 'diseases of power': fascism and Stalinism. One of the numerous reasons why they are, for us, so puzzling, is that in spite of their historical uniqueness they are not quite original. They used and extended mechanisms already in most other societies. More than that: in spite of their own internal madness, they used to a large extent the ideas and the devices of our political rationality. (209)

I mentioned in the Introduction that Foucault believes the relation between rationalization and the excesses of political power to be evident. If we are to avoid the concentration camps and, perhaps even more pertinently a nuclear holocaust, we must embark upon a persistent critique of the notions of autonomy and sovereignty. Yet the resistance is not leveled at rationality *per se*. It is specific rationalities with which we are concerned, and not the process of rationality in general. But how is this to be achieved? Foucault answers: "It consists of taking the forms of resistance against different forms of power as a starting point. To use another metaphor, it consists of using this resistance as a chemical catalyst, so as to bring to light power relations, locate their position, find out their point of application and the methods used" (211).

Foucault has said that three domains of genealogy are possible:

> First, a historical ontology of ourselves in relation to truth through which we constitute ourselves as subjects of knowledge; second, a historical ontology of ourselves in relation to a field of power through which we constitute ourselves as subjects acting on others; third, a historical ontology in relation to ethics through which we constitute ourselves as moral agents. ("Genealogy of Ethics" 351)

So far, in this study, we have been concerned with the examination of the interplay of truth and power, and the constitution of the subject. In the final chapter we will be concerned more directly with the ethical with respect to an adumbration of the notion of "global responsibility."

Deconstruction and Praxis

1. Towards a Global Community

> People who wish to avoid questioning and discussion present deconstruction as a sort of gratuitous chess game with a combination of signs (*combinatoire de signifiants*), closed up in language as in a cave. This misinterpretation is not just a simplification; it is symptomatic of certain political and institutional interests—interests which must also be deconstructed in their turn. I totally refuse the label of nihilism which has been ascribed to me and my American colleagues. Deconstruction is not an enclosure in nothingness, but an openness towards the other. (Kearney 124)

In our discussion so far we have attempted to effect a critique and displacement of metaphysical / technological notions of the human subject by deploying thinkers who seriously / playfully question the primacy of consciousness and its "totalizing" activity. Hopefully, the deconstructive effect has been cumulative. The strategies that we have examined push the notion of rational consciousness further and further from its traditional pre-eminent role in the disclosure of the world. Thus, we have seen that Heidegger's early writings accomplish a reformulation of the Cartesian *cogito* where the existential priority given to *Dasein* broadens the concept of "subjectivity" to include *Dasein's* being-*in*-the-world, rather than standing outside it as an impartial observer. The later writings, we have argued, push the displacing of the primacy of consciousness further by subjecting the constitution of *Dasein* not merely to worldly concern but to the play of time.

Similarly, a parallel move has been made from the Derridean perspective. The Heideggerian insistence on the primacy of language has been taken to a greater extreme in Derrida's thinking. The textualizing of world and subject and the overwhelming pre-occupation with temporal diffusion leave us with a concept of the self, significantly different from that of traditional metaphysics. Part of the efficacy of these deconstructive strategies will depend upon a thorough analysis of the power relations which they intend to disrupt. It is here that Foucault's project (that of providing a genealogical map of such relations) will aid in the production of a political praxis.

In this final Chapter, I will consider some of the effects that our critique might engender in the political sphere. Derrida has argued that in reading any text, all other texts are implicated. I will now argue that the notion of a human subject always implies other human subjects. I will further insist that a global community which respects differences among its members will largely preclude the possibility of ideological conflict and thus render the deployment of nuclear weaponry obsolete. Such a community would also recognize its dependence upon, rather than opposition to, the natural environment within which it coexists. We can no longer afford to construe the other or the ecosystem as an object to be controlled and manipulated according to the dictates of a self-present, sovereign, autonomous and rational subject or a sovereign, autonomous nation-state.

We have already seen that by insisting on the autonomy and sovereignty of consciousness, traditional ontology relegates the other, the "not-self," to the realm of objectivity, to be articulated and controlled according to the dictates of the ego and its rationality. As such, the relationship between self and other is one of violence. This relationship of detachment from the other is to renounce the other and to "enclose oneself within solitude" (Derrida, *Writing and Difference* 91). This solipsistic posture is "neither observation nor sophism; it is the very structure of reason" (91). Thus, traditional metaphysical categories, by construing the self as a pure and simple presence, by renouncing a "certain absence," excludes the other as something to be possessed, seized and known, and "to possess, to know, to grasp are all synonymous of power" (91).

The difficulty, of course, is to think the other as other which, like the problem of thinking the "nature" of *Ereignis*, is exacerbated by the fact that we are confined within a language which privileges one pole of a binary opposition. Consciousness, if it is to retain its ontological priority cannot allow such a transgression. There is, writes Derrida, "no way to conceptualize the encounter" (95). If the knowing is itself power (seizing, grasping), and thus, in a sense, a violence to the other, the intersubjective relation we are after cannot lie in that direction. Perhaps a more efficacious approach would be to argue that the "knowing relation" itself is thoroughly dependent on the existence of the other which both constitutes the possibility of epistemological and ontological inquiries and subsequently limits the possibility of both. We may speak of an "ethical resistance" against the power of consciousness and its categories.

It is from this perspective, Levinas argues, that the ethical relation is to be conceived as prior to any ontological or epistemological relation to the other. In fact, Levinas is prepared to insist that the ethical relation also precedes any notion of a self-relation:

> The ethical exigency to be responsible for the other undermines the ontological primacy of the meaning of Being; it unsettles the natural and political positions we have taken up in the world and predisposes us to a meaning that is other than Being, that is, otherwise than Being (*autrement qu'être*). (Kearney 59)

Such a posture constitutes not merely a dismissal of the primacy of ontology, but also a refusal to privilege the being of myself. My identity and its demands are exploded in my relation with the other. Thus, Levinas argues for an asymmetrical relation "which characterizes the ethical refusal of the first truth of ontology—the struggle to be" (60). We are confronted here with perhaps the most radical displacement of logocentrism, the denial of one's own sovereignty, identity, and autonomy in favor of the other:

> I am defined as a subjectivity, as a singular person, as an 'I' precisely because I am exposed to the other. It is my inescapable and incontrovertible answerability to the other that makes me an individual 'I.' So that I become a responsible or ethical 'I' to the extent that I agree to depose or dethrone myself—to abdicate my position of centrality— in favor of the vulnerable other. (62-63)

But is this response to the other merely a utopian, non-realizable and thoroughly idealistic illusion? Can we effectively deny our ontological being-in-the-world. In his 1981 interview with Levinas, Kearney asks whether in fact such an ethics is practicable in our society (64). Levinas' reply parallels that of Derrida. Just as the deconstructive strategies require that we use and erase our language at one and the same time, so we must "resort to the technico-political systems of means and ends" (64), while at the same time attempting to re-fashion the categories within which political relations have traditionally been thought. Whatever social configurations we may construct in the future, for Levinas, they will be held accountable to this ethical responsibility to the other. In a sense, to speak of ethics as utopian is merely (as Levinas suggests), to point out that this response to the other is "out of place" (*u-topos*) in this world; but then our concern all along has been with the displaced. Levinas' insistence that the ontological inquiry be overturned in favor of the ethical also generates an "ethical resistance" to the epistemological reduction.

The "knowing relation" irrevocably narrows and restricts the possibility of a "non-violent" comportment to the other. When Heidegger speaks of *Gelassenheit*, the letting be of things, he is not merely allowing beings to be "let be" as objects of comprehension, but to be "let be" in their otherness. Of course from the perspective of techno-metaphysics this presents a serious threat: closure is a necessity, openness is anarchy, the possibility of conflict rife. But need aggression follow from the respect of difference? Barthes thinks not:

> Such a society would have no site, could function only in total atopia; yet it would be a kind of phalanstery, for in it contradictions would be acknowledged (and the risks of ideological imposture therefore restricted), difference would be observed, and conflict rendered insignificant. (*Pleasure of the Text* 15)

In terms of the statement that I am attempting to make here, observing difference takes the explicit form of undermining (as we have shown earlier) the notion of autonomy, whether of subject or nation and the notion of sovereignty, whether of consciousness or ideology. This also entails a critique of the societies that have been built upon the fundamental precepts of Western metaphysics.

In "White Mythology," Derrida writes that metaphysics and logocentrism are "white" not only because of their "cold conceptuality" but because they are European white (*Margins of Philosophy*). Deconstruction cannot fail to be a political act, at least (and perhaps much more) inasmuch as it disrupts Western ethnocentrism and exposes Europe / U.S.A. to its other. Deconstruction forces the dominant culture to confront the play of that which is exterior to it, forces it to recognize the marginal. As Caputo has put it, what is being strategically attacked are "the sociological elements" of the metaphysics of presence ("From the Deconstruction of Hermeneutics," an unpublished paper, 10). If part of deconstructive praxis is to show the provisionality of "the powers that be," then part of the task is to show that such structures are in effect, a product, and a product that has a history. This seems to me to be one of the effects of Foucault's genealogical method, as we demonstrated in the last chapter.

"Blood is usually shed in the name of Being, God, or truth, even when and especially when it is shed in the name of 'country,'" Caputo writes. We may have always taken our "fictions" too seriously but now even those fictions are in danger of annihilation. We have not heeded Hegel's warning concerning the inherent partiality of any "knowledge" that purports to capture the whole "truth." I have argued throughout this study that "truth" is not discovered but produced. The most important aspect of the various strategies we have deployed is that they make us remember that we can no longer afford to take ourselves so seriously.

But, how should we take ourselves, or perhaps more pertinently, how should we respond to the other, to otherness? If, as I have argued, deconstruction is not just theory but praxis, what will be the effect of this praxis in the political sphere? Will deconstruction make a difference? It is immensely difficult to formulate positive suggestions from the standpoint of a "position" that is entirely critical. But perhaps, as we noted in the Introduction, this task is less problematic once we realize that the deconstructive posture can only flourish, like any other discourse, because a site has already been opened up. It is the crisis of "modernism" and technological disclosure that generates the manifestation of transgressive discourses such as those of Derrida and Foucault. There is no point arguing that the strategies of "post-modernism" and "post-structuralism" should be consolidated into a coherent and cohesive body of knowledge; this is precisely the danger. If deconstruction is to make the dominant power structures "tremble" it cannot even attempt to "assert" its authority, without itself becoming part of the very establishment it is attempting to displace. There have been occasions where Derrida has been quite specific in arguing that deconstruction does have an affirmative element. In an interview conducted by Richard Kearney in 1981, Kearney asks whether deconstruction can ever "surmount its role of iconoclastic negation and become a form of affirmation?" Derrida replies that

> Deconstruction certainly entails a moment of affirmation. Indeed, I cannot conceive of a radical critique which would not be ultimately motivated by some sort of affirmation, acknowledged or not. Deconstruction always presupposes

affirmation, as I have frequently attempted to point out, sometimes employing a Nietzschean terminology. I do not mean that the deconstructing subject or self affirms. I mean that deconstruction is, in itself, a positive response to an alterity which necessarily calls, summons or motivates it. Deconstruction is therefore vocation—a response to a call. The other, as the other than self, the other that opposes self-identity, is not something that can be detected and disclosed within a philosophical space and with the aid of a philosophical lamp. The other precedes philosophy and necessarily invokes and provokes the subject before any genuine questioning can begin. It is in this rapport with the other that affirmation expresses itself. (Kearney 118)

It is precisely this response, responding, this responsibility to the other, to the marginalized, that we have been suggesting the deconstructive strategies effect. Of course, we have tried to go one step further in arguing that deconstruction has a "vocation" in the political arena *per se*. We have been discussing the possibility of a radical political praxis, but even here Derrida's remarks seem to endorse our argument. Although he admits that he has never been able to directly relate deconstruction to an existing political program, this is not due to the fact that such a relation is precluded because of the nature of his project, but rather, because "the available codes for taking such a political stance are not at all adequate to the radicality of deconstruction" (120). Their lack of adequacy stems from their immersion within traditional philosophical categories; they still remain fundamentally metaphysical, regardless of whether they originate from the "left" or the "right." As with Foucault, Derrida is suspicious of paying lip service to abstract, ideologically infused master-narratives such as that of Marxism. When asked whether deconstruction could be regarded as a disposition (rather than a position) of "responsible anarchy," he responds:

If I had to describe my political disposition I would probably employ a formula of that kind while stressing, of

> course, the interminable obligation to work out and to deconstruct these two terms: 'responsible' and 'anarchy.' If taken as assured certainties in themselves, such terms can also become reified and unthinkable dogmas. But I also try to re-evaluate the indispensable notion of responsibility. (121)

I also take this notion of "responsibility" to be indispensable, albeit, in a form substantially modified from that of the tradition (as in Chapter 1).

I must take it for granted that the threat of nuclear oblivion and / or ecological collapse are in themselves persuasive enough "reasons" for seriously questioning the type of thinking and the presuppositions that have brought them about and brought us to the brink of global annihilation. I have chosen to focus on autonomy and sovereignty because (*vis à vis* global concerns) they appear as both the most prolific and the most pernicious effects of the metaphysics of presence.

The various thinkers that we have considered have one important common concern: the concern with difference. However, I want to insist that the mere embracing of a general pluralism in a world in which difference is not respected will do little to mitigate the effects of our current predicament. We must be careful that the demand for play, innovation and experimentation in the socio-political sphere does not end up in a type of "neo-conservatism" in which "the activation of differences may not amount to a democratic respect of the right of the other to be, but to a conservative plea to place the other, because of her otherness, outside the pale of our common humanity and mutual responsibility" (Kearney 11). But, I would argue, this will only be the case if our concept of the other is presented from the point of view of the *autonomous* subject, with the notions of identity and unity intact. We have, however, shown that the "I" takes place at the intersection of a whole gamut of socio-cultural and political formations. The "I" is thrust forward towards the other in a way that cannot be explicated in terms of any external relation.

A commentator on a paper by Jean-François Lyotard once suggested that it was incumbent upon the latter to provide a "blueprint" of the society of the future, if he expected his critique of "modernism" to be taken seriously. From what we have said above, it must be fairly obvious what it won't look like. The deconstructive attack upon autonomy and sovereignty at the level of the subject works equally well at the level of nations.

Although it may appear that we have wiped the metaphysical slate clean, we cannot and do not live in a vacuum. We could only allow the "play of surfaces" with gay abandonment if it were not the case that the dominant culture threatens to push us into an eternal abyss; this injects a certain urgency into the situation! As Caputo has remarked, "we need a kind of thinking which is at once hermeneutic and deconstructive, both unsettling and recuperative, which exposes us to the abyss but which understands that in that exposure one has reached a deeper understanding of the beings that we are" ("Deconstruction of Hermeneutics 16). Yet, what force is making itself evident in our culture, capable of taking on such a task and being persuasive? I have been arguing throughout this study that the impetus for deploying the deconstructive strategies of certain thinkers is not and cannot be formulated within a political vacuum, for the potentially disastrous consequences of techno-metaphysical disclosure presents us with an immanent problem which cannot be allowed to remain at the theoretical level. The ripples that textual deconstruction engenders cannot fail to be felt in the social body which is itself constituted by the intersection of various texts. The direction in which a political praxis will move will be determined in part by the strategies it deploys. Thus, the insistence on difference and marginality, for example, has a specific target: logocentrism. Similarly, whatever discourse, whether textual or political, that replaces or displaces logocentrism will have to pay due deference to those strategies.

Hal Foster has noted that: "Post-structuralist postmodernism . . . assumes 'the death of man' not only as original creator of unique artifacts but also as the centered subject of representation and of history" ("Post-Modern Polemics" 67). The dispersal of the subject that deconstructive strategies effect is, as I pointed out in the Introduction, not free from political motivation. Fredric Jameson has written that

> The contemporary poststructuralist aesthetic signals the dissolution of the modernist paradigm—with its valorization of myth and symbol, temporality, organic form and the concrete universal, the identity of the subject and the continuity of linguistic expression—and foretells the emergence of some new, properly postmodernist or schizophrenic conception of the artifact—now strategically reformulated as 'text' or *écriture*, and stressing discontinuity, allegory, the mechanical, the gap between signifier and signified, the lapse in meaning, the syncope in the experience of the subject. (*Fables of Aggression* 20)

By textualizing the subject and at the same time releasing the play of signifiers, the inherent liberating after-effect of this gesture, ripples through both the theoretical and practical realm. To use a term of Foster's, the social self becomes "pluralized" and open to a plethora of new configurations (67-68). Furthermore, as Caputo has argued, deconstruction

> is not so much a philosophy of liberation, in the sense of working out a liberationist standpoint, as it is a strategy or praxis of liberation. It is a textual operation performed in the name of, with the intended effect of, liberation; it is not an attempt to work out the theoretical contours of liberation. (14)

Of course we must be careful here not to fall into the hands of a type of neo-conservativism which already mourns the fragmentation of the self as indicative of our era only, as if there was ever a pristine, whole, complete and autonomous subject. But similarly, a response must be offered to those Marxist critics, like Jameson, who would see in deconstruction a perpetuation of the type of fragmentation already indicative of "late-Capitalism."

Because of the resistance against the "totalizing" effect of metaphysics, evident particularly in the writings of Derrida and Foucault, some thinkers (e.g., Habermas, Jay, etc.) have argued for totality, due to the total nature of the nuclear predicament. Thus, we hear this statement from Jay: "That infinite carnivalesque play of which the post-structuralists are so fond may well turn out to be much more suddenly and decisively finite than they or anyone else would desire" (*Marxism and Totality* 536-537). Thus, a nuclear holocaust would be a terminal closure which will demonstrate what the deconstruction of human culture can really mean. Following Jonathan Schell's argument in *Fate of the Earth* that the nuclear peril is global and everlasting, Jay argues that to avoid "the negative totality of nuclear catastrophe" we need a positive totality; we must acknowledge "the complete inter-relatedness of our planetary existence" (536-537). While I endorse Jay's desire for an awareness of our "planetary interrelatedness," I do not believe that the reduction of political strategies to one total and monolithic "party line" will yield the type of society we have been attempting to speak of.

I wish to make it absolutely clear that I have no objection to the deployment of Marx's critique of capitalism and bourgeois political economy. The following remarks constitute a *response* to attacks against deconstruction which would attempt to construe it as an apology for the fragmentation of the subject in the epoch of late capitalism.

Now, I have argued at some length that it is precisely this notion of totalistic thinking that has led to the predicament we now face. It is due to the fact that "techno-metaphysics" refuses to give full recognition to differences, that "inter-relatedness" is precluded. The danger of founding a "total solution" as a response to nuclear war as a total problem is, as Steven Cresap has noted, that "the urgency of the problem may seem to justify excess in the solution. If totality is elevated to the status of our only hope, it gains thereby an ultimacy and authority which might make it very difficult to question those who speak in its favor" (262). Michael Ryan realizes this when he argues that "What is needed . . . is a new form of organization, founded not on guidance, leadership, a knowing elite, and an abstract set of concepts, but instead on participation, self-activity, a diffusion of the leadership function, differences, and radical participatory democracy" (*Marxism and Deconstruction* 203).

It has been the tendency of the rationalist tradition to confuse the notions of "difference" and "opposition." We have seen that from the perspective of deconstruction, *différance* operates in a positive manner, providing for the possibility of conceptuality itself. "Opposition," on the other hand, narrows the openness of this "productive" act, forcing differences to stand one against the other, usually in a relation of master / slave— society / nature, self / other, man / women, etc. There are, however, relations of difference which do not operate according to the binary oppositions of formal systems. The type of relation between human subjects that we have been pursuing is precisely not one that can be reduced to a binary format. That I am distinct from the other does not necessitate that I am opposed to the other nor to otherness *per se*. No reduction to one pole of an artificial dichotomy can exhaust the nature of the place within which I am situated. The boundaries that separate and exclude, demarcate and differentiate, are ideological productions. Not either / or but both / and; this holds true of the relation between self and other selves and of the relation between self and environment. From an ecosystemic viewpoint, subject and planet are always already (*immer schön*) thrown together in a most intricate and complex network of interaction.

The notion of global community need not assume the collapsing of difference, but it cannot accept the existence of the destructive forces that man has launched into the world for this would put difference itself at risk. We are not asking that everyone be the "same" (the latter itself a problematic notion), nor are we arguing that global community requires perceiving ourselves *as* others and others *as* ourselves, but as Cresap argues, "perceiving ourselves *in* others and others *in* ourselves" (262). We need to recognize our inherent interrelatedness without attempting to annul our differences.

One might object that due to the specific and micrological nature of deconstructive strategies, they can be easily subsumed and rendered impotent by the dominating structures of power. This point has been forcefully argued by Jameson:

> These philosophical texts, with their attacks on humanism (Althusser), their celebration of the 'end of man' (Foucault), their ideal of *dissemination* or *dérive* (Derrida, Lyotard), their valorization of schizophrenic writing and schizo-phrenic experience (Deleuze), may in the present context be taken as symptoms of or testimony to a modification of the experience of this subject in consumer or late monopoly capitalism. (*Political Unconscious* 124)

Jameson continues to say that "we may admit the descriptive value of the post-structuralist critique of the 'subject' without necessarily endorsing the schizophrenic ideal it has tended to project" (125). Now, not only is Jameson somewhat cavalier in juxtaposing such a wide variety of philosophical "positions," he also fails to recognize that the subject of the tradition is not displaced in order to be reinvested by, or reconstituted by the psychoanalyst. Decentering the subject is not a matter of engendering confusion in the self but of denying the autonomy and sovereignty of that self. We are not arguing for a sort of "self-imposed" alienation but rather for an awareness that the primacy of consciousness is embedded in a particular social configuration which is now outmoded and pernicious. I think that Foster is right when he argues that

> Here then, we begin to see what is at stake in this so-called dispersal of the subject. For what is this subject that, threatened by loss, is so bemoaned? Bourgeois perhaps, patriarchal certainly—it is the phallocentric order of subjectivity. For some, for many, this is indeed a great loss—and may lead to narcissistic laments about the end of art, of culture, of the West. But for others, precisely for

Others, this is no great loss at all. ("(Post)-Modern
Polemics" 78)

It is only from the perspective of the dominating culture
that such a loss is to be mourned. The fact that, as Seyla Benhabib
has put it, our Faustian dream of "an infinitely malleable world"
is crumbling, is no loss to the marginalized cultures from whom
the dream is a nightmare" ("Epistemologies of Post-Modernism"
105). For the Other, posited against the excesses of Western
rationalism, the classical picture of domination and subordination
(whether of the world's eco-system or of other cultures) is gladly
overturned.

Jameson is correct when he argues that the decentering of
the individual subject can only be achieved by the "emergence of
a post-individualistic social world," only by the inception of a
"new and original form of collective social world" (*Political
Unconscious* 125). But this will not be achieved by re-evoking the
inherently totalizing posture indicative of Western metaphysics.
The imposition of "master-codes," even dialectical ones, will not
do the job. Furthermore, the imposition of master strategies which
ignore the radical differences in the various struggles they attempt
to consolidate has led (historically) to the fragmentation and
diffusion of the power of the left (especially in Britain) to effect
social change. An excessive insistence upon following the "party
line" rather than producing a coherent point of intervention has
resulted in hostile relations between the various groups who each
(inevitably) believe that any "deviation" from *their* line is
tantamount to a counter-revolutionary posture.

One of Jameson's most recurrent grievances, with respect
to deconstruction, is that it somehow neglects the historical
context in which particular texts are generated. It is important to
understand precisely what is meant here by "historical." I have
repeatedly insisted that Derrida's deployment of *différance*, trace,
and other terms has the effect of gesturing toward temporality in
a way that undermines the tradition's preoccupation with
presence. However, (and I think this is Jameson's objection)
deconstruction does not rely upon placing the text within a

particular historical period which is in itself clearly delineated; in fact, deconstruction flatly denies the periodization that is evident in most Marxist critiques of history. Thus, Jameson can argue that

> the impulse behind the critical practice [of deconstruction] . . . brackets the historical situations in which texts are effective and insists that ideological positions can be identified by the identification of inner-textual or purely formal features. Such an approach is thereby able to confine its work to individual printed texts, and projects the a-historical view that the formal features in question always and everywhere bear the same ideological change. (283)

Two points seem pertinent here. First, to speak about a distinction between form and content is already to have presupposed that such a binary opposition is in place. Notions such as "representation," "narrative closure," "centered subject," or "presence," are no more "formal" than are Jameson's predilection to speak of "contradiction," "class struggle," and particular historical periods. In each case there is a desire to generate a specific field of inquiry, to unmask a specific set of ideological complicities, or so it would seem at first glance. However, if we look a little closer we notice that deconstructive strategies do indeed "unmask" the existence of metaphysical categories and attempt to displace them, whereas Marxism insists on imposing its categories which it deems necessary for a realization of the historical situatedness of its data. Furthermore, it seems hardly surprising that given the pervasiveness of metaphysical categories, including that of opposition, that deconstruction unearths the same ideological underpinnings in all the texts it encounters. Deconstruction does not shirk the need to "situate" texts within the extrinsic or situational references because, as we have said above, the opposition between intrinsic and extrinsic, text and reality, has been displaced.

Jameson's criticisms would be more pertinent were they levelled at structuralism rather than deconstruction. For the deconstructionist, signs achieve meaning not merely by their opposition to other signs at the synchronic level but by a referral to signs and signifying chains that are no longer present. I am aware that, as Jameson argues, periodization is only problematic if one insists on imputing to Marxism a vulgar mechanistic construal of periodization. Yet, a more sophisticated treatment of history, one that recognizes that history is opaque rather than transparent and self-articulating (given that it only comes to us in textualized form), that is, a view of history as an "absent cause," a text-to-be-created, is closer to the deconstructionist's "position" than Jameson is prepared to admit.

While most deconstructive interventions have been specific and piecemeal, the larger issues have been ignored, especially those dealing with socio-political problems, the addressing of those problems is not precluded but merely neglected; this study is itself an attempt to remedy such neglect. Furthermore, given that the dominant structure is dependent upon a veritable plethora of discursive formations, interconnected yet having their origin in a wide range of diverse micro-structures, an over-arching and holistic resistance is unlikely to be effective. There cannot be merely one strategy, and even if there were such a possibility, it would run the risk of sedimentation and would be susceptible to nullification by the dominant structure.

To what extent these post-industrial options can be fully explicated cannot be foretold in advance but we might be in a position to pave the way by correctly analyzing the more pernicious aspects of the current power relations that constitute industrial cultures. Lyotard is undoubtedly correct, as we have seen more explicitly in our consideration of Foucault's genealogical method, that such cultures fuse the concepts of power and knowledge. Of course, Foucault does not see this relation as a limitation, and it is probably true that he would not take seriously any attempt to transcend it, but as I have stressed earlier, Foucault's genealogies are useful maps of power relations rather than predictions for future social configurations. Lyotard argues that "Power . . . legitimates science and the law on the basis of their efficiency, and legitimates this efficiency on the basis of science and the law. . . . Thus the growth of power, and its self-legitimation are now taking the route of data storage and accessibility, and the operativity of information" (*Postmodern Condition* 47). Lyotard endorses what we have seen from Heidegger and Derrida; the paradigm of language has replaced the paradigm of consciousness.

Of course, we are not suggesting that it is possible to dispense with the subject. Derrida is very clear on this point:

> To deconstruct the subject does not mean to deny its existence. There are subjects, 'operations' or 'effects' (*effets*) of subjectivity. This is an incontrovertible fact. To acknowledge this does not mean, however, that the subject is what it says it is. The subject is not some meta-linguistic substance or identity, some pure *cogito* of self-presence; it is always inscribed in language. My work does not, therefore, destroy the subject; it simply tries to resituate it. (Kearney 125)

In part this has been my aim in this study.

In conclusion, I would agree that one needs to be very wary of those who would see in deconstruction a type of political paralysis. I believe Ryan to be correct when he argues that "only from the viewpoint of capitalist rationalism or party patriarch-alism does the persistent positing of an alternative, of a continuous displacement along a seriality of revolutions which is multi-sectoral and without conclusion, seem 'irrational' or 'paralytic'" (214). Global annihilation is a very real possibility while nations tenaciously attempt to protect their identity in the belief that they are guarding something precious and essential. We have shown both the basis for this obsession and shown it to be a dangerous chimera. "Only from the point of view of power, authority, and identity do difference and diversity seem dangerous" (Ryan 216).

If as I believe Ryan is right in concluding that "ideology is the political use of metaphysics in the domain of practice" and that "ideology is always inscribed in material structures of force" (216), then we must carry through the critique of of the metaphysics of presence to a critique of ideological imposture. Despite the fact that many of its opponents have seen deconstruction as necessarily undermining the notion of "value," it might well be the case that the deconstructive posture of radical questioning is of itself the "highest value." Our planet is not threatened by tolerance nor by insisting that the marginal have a voice; planetary destruction demands a certain singularity of purpose and the practioners of deconstruction can hardly be accused of that!

2. Modes of Intervention

If we are to avoid the totalizing impetus of master narratives and certain forms of utopian rationalizations the strategies that we deploy must be heterogeneous. In this final section I would like to consider two forms of intervention: Gregory Ulmer's recent application of grammatology to pedagogy and my own attempt to formulate a provisional structure of social organization based upon a political deployment of metonymy. Ulmer writes that

> theoretical fictions organized into a pedagogy that would collapse the distinctions separating teaching, research, and art might also have the power to guide transformations of the lived social world. (*Applied Grammatology* 27)

Given Lyotard's warning, that the growth of power is now inextricably linked to what he terms the "operativity of information," serious consideration to the way that information is disseminated and received cannot be avoided, without significantly reducing the effect of our deconstructive strategies. New pedagogical techniques, which undermine the authoritorial posture of the academy, are as important politically as the more direct forms of intervention.

Ulmer has discerned in Derrida's writings, not merely a negative moment, but also a moment of affirmation. The decompostional element is merely one side. Grammatology constitutes a compositional methodology, and one that provides an alternative *modus operandi* to logocentric binary oppositions, operative in the realm of pedagogy.

> Theoretical grammatology . . . is a repetition, a retracing at a conceptual level, of the history of writing. Its purpose is

to disentangle in that history the nature (or the absence of an essence) of writing from the ideology or metaphysics of voice which has dominated and restricted writing in order to reassess the full potential of, and alternative directions for, a new writing practice. (68)

We have already discussed in Chapter Two of Part I, the Heideggerian project which, in its destruction of onto-theology, attempts a new experience with language; appropriate to thinking the "nature" or *Ereignis*. Derrida hopes to effect a similar operation with regard to *différance*, by a displacement of the phoneme; allowing the play of the grapheme to function within an open syntactic network. Thus, as Ulmer points out, Derrida generates a "graphic rhetoric" which is "a double-valued Writing, ideographic and phonetic at once" (98). Like Heidegger's use of everyday speech in strange configurations, it is not Derrida's intention to create a new language, but to transform the one we have and make it tremble (*ébranler*). Given, as we have argued all along, that metaphysical postulates are inherently tied up with our current technological *Gestell*, the communication techniques for the dissemination of information are equally bound by logocentric categories. Any shift away from the tradition's binding grammatical restraints will covariantly displace the production and reception of information. Pedagogically, the classroom becomes, as Ulmer notes, "a place of intervention rather than reproduction" (164). Now, of course, it might be argued, that this project does not seem dissimilar to the "progressive" schools of the "sixties," in both Europe and the United States. However, there is one significant difference—rather than attempting a clean break with the establishment, grammatology would unfold its double pronged attack within the institution, and not present a detached alternative.

An application of grammatology to teaching . . . involves a rethinking of the 'space' in which the discourse of ideas takes place. Given that grammatological presentations are neither reproductions of reality nor revelations of the real, it is clear that grammatology involves a displacement of educational transmissions from the domain of truth to that of invention. (179)

Ulmer elicits certain points which could outline the nature of this new pedagogy. First, we must recognize that the type of intervention we are suggesting well be directed toward the whole educational system, and from the inside. Second, Derrida's theory of writing can be construed as a "new rhetoric of intervention," and thus, "Writing becomes a research into all processes of innovation and change" (228-229). Third, we have the construction of models which will serve to overthrow the domination of phonocentrism: thus, Derrida's exploration of a new hieroglyphic writing, supplementing verbal discourse with ideographic and pictorial elements. Perhaps the most important characteristic of the new pedagogy is that which Ulmer designates as "autography." It is here that the question of the subject of knowledge is raised. The site of authority which usually invests the teacher must be displaced in favor of an open-ended play of information. Of course, what is being attempted here is a dismantling of the distinction between the academy and the general public—popularization. This exploding of the inner sanctum may help the perpetuation of an intertextuality of discourses, reducing the hierarchical ranking of discursive formations. Thus, the centers of domination become dispersed along a metonymic chain, eroding their claim to mastery.

> The organizing principle of applied grammatology may be simply stated . . . hieroglyphics. The hieroglyph emblematizes Derrida's lesson for didactic discourse, including its association with dephoneticization. . . . The import of the hieroglyph as an emblem of the new pedagogy is that teaching must include in its considerations the non-discursive and linguistic dimensions of thought and communication. (228)

Contrary to the metaphysical desire to hierarchically rank discourses, grammatology would situate discursive formations according to varieties of contiguity, combination, and contexture. On a global level this might be effected (given radical changes in current power relations) by the intervention of micro-technology in the area of information transmission. Cage's dream (Woodward) of a global society where electronics is conceived as a "spiritual" force harnessed in the service of a radical participatory democracy is close in its political vision to many deconstructionist writers concerned to tentatively explore the praxis that might be forthcoming from the theoretical advances of deconstructive critical inquiry. Of course, whether post-industrial technology, especially in the area of electronic communication, would aid in the transformation of hierarchies of power / knowledge into democratized horizontal networks, a sort of social expression of the Derridean overturning and displacement of philosophical hierarchies, or would merely reaffirm the rationalist paradigm of atomic individualism is open to debate. Measures would have to be taken to guard against isolationism. There would be a need to promote the use of the system by collectives rather than individuals.

It does seem clear that this proposal remains totally naive unless there is an increased resistance to the operations of the multi-national corporations that presently control such technology. At present the dominating force which controls the production and distribution of global resources is profit. The operations of the multi-nationals, themselves the apotheosis of Western rationalism, determine not merely the economic relations between human beings but also promote cultural values antithetical to community. The criminal lack of concern for the integrity of the global ecosystem, evident in the pillaging of Third World resources (both natural and human) must be overcome— the Western paradigm of infinite economic expansion must be exposed, revealing its deleterious effects on our environment.

Anthony Wilden's reformulation of Bateson's model, depicting the relations of "biosocial imperialism" may be useful here.

FIGURE 1 *The Relationships of Biosocial Imperialism*

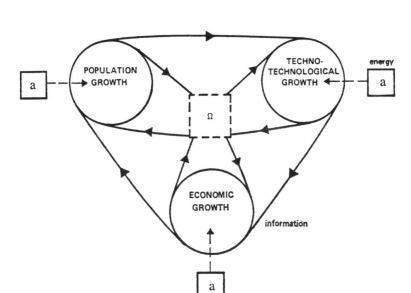

NATURAL RESOURCES (DECREASING)   WASTE (INCREASING)
—INFORMATION LINKAGES (Clockwise = Positive Feedback)

a	FREE ENERGY NEGENTROPY FLEXIBILITY	BOUND ENERGY ENTROPY INFLEXIBILITY

(Wildon 209)

The "a" factor mirrors the "operation" of *différance* which is negentropic in that it increases the possibility of new structures within the global ecosystem thus ensuring flexibility, a necessary ingredient of our survival.

As both Marx and Wilden have pointed out, the combination of rationalism and capitalism when equipped with
modern technological tools can have a devastating effect on the
global ecosystem:

> Our industrial culture has traditionally depended upon an
> 'ethic of disposability' for which natural resources, other
> people's ecosystems—'other' human beings in general and
> the disposable beer can have had roughly the same
> exchange value. (Wilden 207)

However, if such resistance were to be effective, the
transformation of hierarchies could be facilitated or at least aided
by modes of electronic communication—horizontal networks
with no center, no apex of authority. What is being suggested
could be construed as a type of global syndicalism with advanced
forms of telecommunications as its impetus. Democratic access to
these networks would be ensured by a standardized technology.
With increasing standardization on a global scale there would be
less room for the domination of specialists, thus breaking the
imperialistic technocracy.

Just as *différance* defies any attempts to privilege any one
ultimate focus or single point of reference for the signifying
process, so our provisional global community would involve an
interlacing of disparate centers of cultural activity. Having
displaced the *arche* or teleological demands of Western
rationalism, there would exist no over-arching ideological goal to
which subjects would unquestioningly give allegiance. Such an
arrangement would increase flexibility in political organization as
well as disrupting the pernicious interrelations between
epistemology, ideology and economics.

If one's dreams are to be effective, the strategies developed
to achieve them must take into consideration current power
configurations. Resistance against the centralized control of world
capital must be waged simultaneously from the center (the
industrialized West) and from the margins (the so-called
underdeveloped nations) with a plethora of tactical and strategic

interventions. We must be careful not to fall back into an ethnocentric posture in which the determination of meaning and significance in our organized planetary culture is the single privilege of an advanced technocratic elite.

Given that the most pernicious effects of our present global political arrangements such as nuclear proliferation, ecological devastation and world hunger require a global solution, it is necessary that some form of central organization exist to oversee and ensure nuclear disarmament, equitable re-distribution of the Earth's resources and provide a means of monitoring the effects of technology on the global eco-system.

The most efficacious form of tactical intervention and one consistent with the theoretical underpinnings of this study would be civil disobedience. There is enough evidence to suggest that such action can be effective both in those areas where mass resistance is essential, as against the military / industrial complex, and on a local level such as occupying factories which are about to be closed by multi-national corporations seeking higher profits in the Third World. The project is to make the policies of those in power unworkable. While it would be necessary to form a central organization to consolidate action upon a particular issue, policy decisions would be taken at the local level subject to the needs and conditions of local communities. This need to keep the centers of powers localized is particularly important to ensure that Third World communities have the opportunities to fully control decision making procedures which directly affect them. It is extremely arrogant (not to mention imperialistic) to believe that the industrialized world can speak for the non-industrialized countries; one need only observe the appalling crimes that have been carried out under the guise of the "green revolution."

We must radically alter the present relationship between the industrial / military complex (headed by the multi-national corporations) and our biosocial environment—the Earth. This situation must be reversed if we are to survive. A planetary culture organized along global syndicalist lines would increase flexibility in our relations with others and in our relations with our environment, stimulating greater possibilities for the growth of non-exploitative technologies and political systems.

The above suggestions in no way present an exhaustive "blue-print" of what the displacement of logocentrism might engender. I would hope that the study as a whole might be taken seriously enough to stimulate discussion within postmodern discourse, which, I believe, has been somewhat reticent in addressing the practical possibilities of its own reflections.

List of Works Cited

Arac, Jonathan and Wlad Godzich, eds. *The Yale Critics: Decon-struction in America.* Minneapolis: University of Minnesota Press, 1983.

Bataille, Georges. *Das Theoretische Werk.* Vol. 7. Munich: Rogner and Bernhard, 1975.

Barthes, Roland. *S/Z.* Trans. Richard Miller. New York: Hill and Wang, 1974.

_____. *Pleasure of the Text.* Trans. Richard Miller. New York: Hill and Wang, 1975.

Benhabib, Seyla. "Epistemologies of Post-Modernism." *New German Critique* 33 (1984): 103-126.

Caputo, John, "From the Deconstruction of Hermeneutics to the Hermeneutics of Deconstruction." Unpublished at the time of this writing.

Conby, Tom. "A Trace of Style." *Displacement.* Ed. Mark Krupnick. Bloomington: Indiana University Press, 1983.

Cornay, D. B. "Kant and the Closure of the Epoch of the Metaphysics of Presence." *Southwest Journal of Philosophy* (1979): 39-72.

Cresap, Steven. "Review" *New German Critique* 33 (1984): 257-263.

De Man, Paul. *Allegories of Reading: Figural Language in Rousseau, Nietzsche, Rilke, and Proust.* New Haven: Yale University Press, 1979.

Derrida, Jacques. *Dissemination.* Trans. Barbara Johnson. Chicago: University of Chicago Press, 1981.

_____. *Of Grammatology.* Trans. Gayatri Spivak. Baltimore: Johns Hopkins University Press, 1974.

_____. *Margins of Philosophy.* Trans. Alan Bass. Chicago: University of Chicago Press, 1982.

_____. *Speech and Phenomena and Other Essays on Husserl's*

Theory of Signs. Trans. David B. Allison. Evanston: Northwestern University Press, 1973.

_____. *Writing and Difference.* Trans. Alan Bass. Chicago: University of Chicago Press, 1978.

Descartes, René. *The Philosophical Works of Descartes.* 2 vols. Trans. Elizabeth Haldane and George Ross. Cambridge: Cambridge University Press, 1984.

Dreyfus, Hubert. "Beyond Hermeneutics: Interpretation in Late Heidegger and Recent Foucault." *Hermeneutics.* Ed. Gary Shapiro. Amherst: University of Massachusettes Press, 1984. 66-83.

Foster, Hal. "(Post)Modern Polemics." *New German Critique* 33 (1984): 67-78.

Foucault, Michel. *Archaeology of Knowledge.* Trans. A. M. Sheridan Smith. New York: Pantheon Books, 1984.

_____. *Discipline and Punish: The Birth of the Prison.* Trans. Alan Sheridan. New York: Vintage Books, 1979.

_____. *Foucault Reader.* Ed. Paul Rabinow. New York: Pantheon Books, 1984.

_____. *The History of Sexuality.* Trans. Robert Hurley. New York: Pantheon Books, 1980.

_____. *Language, Counter-Memory, Practice: Selected Essays and Interviews.* Trans. and ed. Donald F. Bouchard. Ithaca: Cornell University Press, 1977.

_____. *The Order of Things: An Archeology of the Human Sciences.* New York: Vintage Books, 1973.

_____. *Power/Knowledge: Selected Interviews and Other Writings.* Trans. Colin Gordan. New York: Pantheon Books, 1980.

_____. *Use of Pleasure.* Trans. Robert Hurley. New York: Pantheon Books, 1985.

_____. "Afterword: The Subject and Power." *Michel Foucault.* Ed. Hubert Dreyfus. Chicago: University Press, 1983.

_____. "On the Genealogy of Ethics: an Overview of Work in Progress." *Foucault Reader.* Ed. Paul Rabinow. New York: Pantheon Books, 1984. 340-372.

_____. "Politics and Ethics: An Interview." *Foucault Reader.* Ed.

Paul Rabinow. New York: Pantheon Books, 1984. 373-380.

Fraser, Nancy. "The French Derrideans: Politicizing Deconstruction or Deconstructing the Political." *New German Critique* 33 (1984): 127-154.

Gasche, Rudolphe. "Joining the Text." *The Yale Critics: Deconstruction in America*. Eds. Jonathan Arac and Wlad Godzich. Minneapolis: University of Minnesota Press, 1983. 156-175.

Habermas, Jürgen. "The French Path of Modernity." *New German Critique* 33 (1984): 79-102.

Harries, Karsten. "Fundamental Ontology and the Search of Man's Place." *Heidegger and Modern Philosophy*. Ed. M. Murray. New Haven: Yale University Press, 1978. 65-79.

Heidegger, Martin. *Being and Time*. Trans. John Macquarrie and Edward Robinson. Oxford: Blackwell, 1978.

_____. *Basic Writings from Being and Time to the Task of Thinking*. Trans. and ed. David F. Krell. New York: Harper and Row, 1977.

_____. *Discourse on Thinking*. Trans. John M. Anderson and E. Hans Freund. New York: Harper and Row, 1966.

_____. *The End of Philosophy*. Trans. Joan Stambaugh. New York: Harper and Row, 1973.

_____. *On the Way to Language*. Trans. Peter D. Hertz. New York: Harper and Row, 1977.

_____. "Wesen and Begriff der Physis: Aristotles, Physik B, 1." Trans. Thomas Sheehan. *Man and World* 9 (1976): 219-270. (English title, "On Being and Conception of Physis in Aristotle's Physics B, 1.")

Jameson, Fredric. *Fables of Aggression: Wyndham Lewis, the Modernist as Fascist*. Berkeley: University of California Press, 1979.

_____. *The Political Unconscious: Narrative as Socially Symbolic Act*. Ithaca: Cornell University Press, 1981.

Jay, Martin. *Marxism and Totality: The Adventure of a Concept from Lukacs to Habermas*. Berkelely: University of California Press, 1984.

Kearney, Richard. *Dialogues with Contemporary Continental Thinkers: The Phenomenological Heritage: Paul Ricoeur, Emmanual Levinas, Herbert Marcuse, Stanislas Breton, Jacques Derrida*. Manchester, UK and Dover, NH: Manchester University Press, 1984.

Kisiel, Theodore. "The Language of the Event: The Event of Language." *Heidegger and the Path of Thinking*. Pittsburg: Duquense University Press, 1970. 85-104.

Krell, David. "Introductory Comments." *Martin Heidegger: Basic Writings*. New York: Harper and Row, 1977.

Krupnick, Mark, ed. *Displacement: Derrida and After*. Bloomington: Univeristy of Indiana Press, 1983.

Lyotard, Jean-François. *The Postmodern Condition: A Report on Knowledge*. Trans. Geoff Bennington and Brian Massumi. Minneapolis: University of Minnesota Press, 1984.

Macherey, Pierre. *A Theory of Literary Production*. Trans. Geoffrey Wall. London and Boston: Routledge & Kegan Paul, 1978.

Mitchell, W. J. T. *The Politics of Interpretation*. Chicago: University of Chicago Press, 1983.

Nietzsche, Friedrich. *The Will to Power*. Trans. Walter Kaufmann and R. J. Hollingdale. New York: Vintage Books, 1968.

_____. *The Complete Works of Nietzsche*. Ed. Oscar Levy. New York: 1964.

_____. *The Gay Science*. Trans. Walter Kaufmann. New York: Vintage Books, 1974.

_____. *Beyond Good and Evil*. Trans. R. J. Hollingdale. Hammondsworth and Baltimore: Penguin Books, 1973.

Poeggler, Otto. "Being as Appropriation." *Heidegger and Modern Philosophy*. Ed. M. Murray. New Haven: Yale University Press, 1978. 84-115.

Richardson, William. "Heidegger's Way Through Phenomenology to the Thinking of Being." *Listening: Journal of Religion and Culture* (1977): 21-37.

Ricoeur, Paul. *Conflict of Interpretation: Essays in Hermeneutics*. Ed. Don Ihde. Evanston: Northwestern University Press. 1974.

Ryan, Michael. *Marxism and Deconstruction*. Baltimore: Johns Hopkins University Press, 1982.

Saussure, Ferdinand de. *Course in General Linguistics.* Trans. Wade Baskin. New York: McGraw-Hill, 1966.

Schell, Jonathon. *The Fate of the Earth.* New York: Avon Books, 1982.

Schurmann, Reiner. "The Ontological Difference and Political Philosophy." *Philosophy and Phenomenological Research.* (1979): 99-122.

_____. "Questioning the Foundation of Practical Philosophy." *Phenomenology: Dialogues and Bridges.* E. Ronald Bruzina. Albany: State University of New York Press, 1982. 11-21.

Sheehan, Thomas. "On the Way to *Ereignis*: Heidegger's Interpretation of Physis." *Continental Philosophy in America.* Pittsburg: Duquense University Press, 1983.

Schuwer. A. "Prolegomena to Time and Being: Truth and Time." *Heidegger and the Path of Thinking.* Pittsburg: Duquense University Press, 1970. 169-190.

Spivak, Gayatri. "Preface to *Of Grammatology.*" Baltimore: Johns Hopkins University Press, 1974.

Ulmer, Gregory. *Applied Grammatology: Post(e)-Pedagogy from Jacques Derrida to Joseph Beuys.* Baltimore: Johns Hopkins University Press, 1985.

White, Hayden. "The Politics of Historical Interpretation: Discipline and De-Sublimation." *The Politics of Interpretation.* Ed. W J. T. Mitchell. Chicago: University of Chicago Press, 1983. 119-144.

Wilden, Anthony. *System and Structure: Essays in Communication and Exchange.* 2nd edition. London and New York: Tavistock Publications, 1980.

Woodward, Kathleen, ed. *The Myths of Information: Technology and Postindustrial Culture.* Madison, WI: Coda Press, 1980.

Index

Parmenides, 16
Phanesthai (appearances), 17
Phonocentrism: *see* Derrida and phonocentrism
Plato: metaphysics of, 17
Play: *see* Derrida and play
Poeggler, Otto, 16
Poetry: *see* Heidegger and poetry
Politics: *see* deconstruction as radical critique
Polysemy, 3
Postmodernism, 96, 99
Post-structuralism, 7, 54-58, 96, 99-101
Power, 102, 106-107, 114-115; *see also* knowledge and power; Foucault and power
Presence, metaphysics of: *see* Logocentrism
Prison: *see* Foucault and punishment

Rabbinic Thought: *see* Derrida and the rabbinic tradition
Rationalism: *see* Enlightenment
Reason, the Age of: *see* Enlightenment
Releasement: *see* Heidegger and releasement
Representation: *see* Foucault and Heidegger and representation
Resemblance: in Renaissance thought, 20
Resistance, 86-90, 95-108, 111-115
Richardson, William, 34-35
Ricoeur: and interpretation of Heidegger, 36-38
Ryan, Michael, 107

Saussure, Ferdinand de, 51-57

Schell, Jonathon, 101
Schurman, Reiner, 35, 47
Schuwer, A., 46
Sexuality: *see* Foucault and sexuality
Sheehan, Thomas, 22
Speech: *vs* writing, *see* Derrida and writing
Spivak, Gayatri, 2, 25, 56-57
Stoics: and ethics, 30-31
Structuralism: defined, 51
Subjectivity: rationalist conception, 24-25; deconstructed, 26-28; *see also* Heidegger and *Dasein*
Syndicalism: global, 114
Systemization, 20-21

Technology, 2, 9, 27, 91, 96, 99, 113-115; *see also* Heidegger and technology
Time, 16, 18, 100-101, 106
Truth, 18-20, 24, 26, 31, 63, 77-79, 90

Ulmer, Gregory, 109-111
Utopia: as atopos, 94

Violence: and traditional ontology, 92

White, Hayden, 86
Wilden, Anthony, 112-114
Will to Knowledge, 24
Will to Power, 73
Will to Truth, 73

Woodward, Kathleen, 112
Writing: and Judaism, 58-60; *see also* Derrida and writing

Keith C. Pheby holds the Ph.D. in philosophy from Marquette University, specializing in 20th century European philosophy. He has taught philosophy at Iowa State University and Marquette. Out of concern for the continuing threat of nuclear confrontation, Dr. Pheby has returned to Europe (where he was born in 1952) to devote more of his time to political interventions in support of peace movements. Dr. Pheby is also writing another book on the aesthetics of the body—an articulation of the non-cognitive interactions of bodies as a "model" for social and political interaction. He currently resides in Hereford, West Midlands, England.